Biblical Insight for COPING WITH CHAOS

by
Robert W. Ellison

Copyright © 2008 by Robert W. Ellison

Biblical Insight for COPING WITH CHAOS
by Robert W. Ellison

Printed in the United States of America

ISBN 978-1-60477-923-3

All rights reserved solely by the author. The author guarantees all contents are original and do not infringe upon the legal rights of any other person or work. No part of this book may be reproduced in any form without the permission of the author. The views expressed in this book are not necessarily those of the publisher.

Unless otherwise indicated, Bible quotations are taken from The King James Version of the Bible. Copyright © 1976 by Thomas Nelson Publishers.

www.xulonpress.com

DEDICATION

*This book is dedicated to the memory and legacy
of
the Reverend "T. B." Ellison
Beloved father, friend, and confidant
whose life and witness have inspired many.
Who through perseverance, and tireless devotion
to God and family, has left a legacy of faith
that is sure to transcend the generations to come.
We shall all miss him greatly.*

CONTENTS

Acknowledgments ix

Introduction xi

Chapter One: *All Boxed In* 13

Chapter Two: *The Birth of Chaos* 37

Chapter Three: *Identity Crisis* 45

Chapter Four: *Chaos and the Prodigal Son* 59

Chapter Five: *The Benefits of Wisdom* 81

Chapter Six: *The Stewardship of Time* 105

Chapter Seven: *The Importance of Prayer* 123

Chapter Eight: *The Planting Season* 137

Chapter Nine: *Chaos and the Power of the Tongue* 149

Chapter Ten: *The Specter of Spiritual Warfare* 157

ACKNOWLEDGMENTS

It is altogether fitting and proper, that those who inspired and assisted in the preparation of this book, be acknowledged for their invaluable assistance, which helped to make this all possible. To my loving wife Rhonda, who has always inspired and believed in me, and has been a constant "cheerleader" throughout this endeavor, my love and sincere thanks to you. To my beloved mother, Francina, whose support and spiritual strength has been a constant throughout my life. To my sister Deborah, whose teaching abilities and love for God, has challenged me to pursue excellence in disseminating the Word of God. And finally, to Cindy Rosales Cooper, my sincere thanks for time spent in your editorial assistance of this project.

Of course, I would be remiss, if I failed to acknowledge the One who is responsible for making *all* things possible, my Lord and Savior, Jesus Christ. For He has given me the desires of my heart, and they are for the expansion of His Kingdom as a result of this work.

Amen

INTRODUCTION

When confronted with chaotic or adverse situations, there is a natural tendency to seek solace or comfort. The intended goal is to alleviate pain or stress, whether it be physical, emotional, or spiritual. We try to avoid stress-producing components in our lives, simply because they appear to be non-beneficial, and seem to work more to our detriment than to our well-being. We often feel that as long as some degree of "calm" can be maintained in the midst of our circumstances, at least some form of contentment is likely to follow. This level of contentment is generally referred to as a "comfort zone." This zone can relate to either the physical, emotional, or spiritual arena.

Oftentimes, we find contentment in a particular situation, and satisfactorily maintain a "status quo" mentality, never really preparing for the unexpected to happen. These are the times of "chaos," when life itself is interrupted by the infusion of the unexpected. Chaos materializes in many forms, some of which include: natural disasters, the unexpected death of a loved one, prodigal children, loss of income, a long-term illness, and even the rejection of truth. Chaos, from its very root, is defined as disorder; confusion, or disarray and has an air of unpredictability.

While this book could not possibly cover every aspect of chaos, the intended purpose in this writing is to bring to the attention of the reader certain key areas of life where chaotic circumstances have been known to manifest, and how to confront these situations while being victorious in the process. The reality is that life has the propensity of being unpredictable, and as such, imposes limits on our comfort zones. When this takes place, we find ourselves being placed in positions of change, which could either yield positive or negative results. Either way, change is inevitable!

When change occurs, we are catapulted from the mundane complexities of life in order that we may experience the awesome life changing power of God! It was God who brought order out of chaos in the beginning of creation, and He has established order through His Son, in this season of chaos that we now face.

CHAPTER ONE

ALL BOXED IN

"Yea, they turned back and tempted God, and limited the Holy One of Israel." (Psalms 78:41)

Have you ever wondered what it would be like to live life inside of a box? Of course, many of us would not entertain the thought, but there are those less fortunate, that sometimes depend on boxes for shelter. A "box" according to Webster's definition is, "a rigid typically rectangular receptacle, often with a cover." When used in a verbal format, the definition reads, "to enclose in."

The meaning is significant, because it helps to identify the correlation of the conventional meaning of the word, in respect to the way in which some of us are prone to live our lives. For instance, in the literal sense, a box is used to enclose or "contain" something. The contained object is limited to the parameters *inside of the box*, thereby restricting the movement of that object to the *confines* of the box. Keeping this concept in mind, think of your own limitations in relation to your comfort zone. As long as you are *inside* the confines of the "box" (or zone), you are most likely to feel compelled to relax somewhat; thereby shifting your focus on everything inside the confines of the box. But what's taking place *outside* of the box? Do we dare explore? In most instances, we do not; that is, until adversity strikes!

LIMITING GOD

All too often, we try to limit God to our little "box." God cannot be contained, nor will He be manipulated to serve our purposes. The Israelites learned this lesson the hard way at the battle of Aphek (I Samuel 4:1-2). They viewed the Ark of the Covenant as a representation of God, Himself. It appeared that they took on a superstitious view concerning the situation; by believing that the power of God was contained within the ark. What a grave mistake! God's judgment of His people resulted in the slaughter of thousands, at the hands of the Philistines. Not only were they defeated in battle, but God allowed the ark to be captured, and taken away from the camp of the Israelites. This was a devastating blow, as the ark was "symbolic" of God's presence within the camp. It didn't mean that the ark itself was God. The illustration is to show that God cannot be confined to a "box." In doing so, the Israelites placed limitations on the power of God. Had they even attempted to call out to God in prayer, no doubt He would have responded to their dilemma. *"If thou afflict them in any wise, and they cry at all unto me, I will surely hear their cry"* (Exodus 22:23). Instead, they chose to respond to their enemy with the same polytheistic, superstitious mindset as the people they were fighting!

The Almighty God of glory will not be used to serve the purposes of man. He is the Creator of all things, and sustains all of life. The very foundations of the world were framed by the *power* of His spoken Word! "He hath made the earth by his power, he hath established the world by his wisdom, and hath stretched out the heaven by his understanding" (Jeremiah 51:15). Such power could never be relegated to any man-made structure, however; God did give specific instructions to Moses in the building of the Ark of the Covenant. It was to carry the two stone tablets listing the Ten Commandments, along with some other covenant promises of God.

Keep in mind, during the time of the Old Testament, God chose to relate to man in a different manner from which He does today. Because Christ had not yet come to the earth (in bodily form), and the Holy Spirit did not appear until after Christ, God communicated in a variety of ways that was rarely predictable. Whether it was audible, as He did with Moses by way of a burning bush (Exodus 3:4), through an animal as with Balaam (Numbers 22:28), by way of His angelic hosts (Hebrews 1:14), or through dreams and visions as recorded in Daniel 1 v. 17, God had an arresting way of getting one's attention.

When we limit the awesome power of God in our lives, we are cheating ourselves out of a great deal of our inheritance. You may ask "how exactly do we limit God's power?" The answer is by simply denying it, or refusing to believe that it can work for you. Jesus, Himself was limited in His effectiveness at the beginning of His ministry. Why? It was because of the **inability** of the townspeople to believe in His anointed power for ministry. "And he could there do no mighty work, save that he laid his hands upon a few sick folk, and healed them" (Mark 6:5). It was because of their unbelief, the Bible says, that Jesus marveled. He could not believe their disbelief!

Have you ever tried to explain something to someone, the very best way that you knew how, and yet they still couldn't grasp what you were saying? Frustrating, isn't it? There are some people, as well meaning as they are, that are simply locked in on one train of thought; never open to new ideas or even willing to entertain the thought of new possibilities. As long as they remain "fixed" in that mode, they will remain in the confines of a "boxed in" lifestyle. Business as usual will be the order of the day, never opening up to the infinite possibilities in life that Jesus has already made provision for. This is the very attitude that defeats most Christians in their spiritual walk. Because of unbelief, they are cheating themselves out of their spiritual inheritance. If you are blinded to the rights of your inheritance, what could you possibly expect to gain?

INHERITANCE OF THE COVENANT

In Genesis 17, God made a covenant with Abraham. Contained in that covenant, God promised that because of Abraham's faith and obedience that his seed would be blessed, and that in his seed all the nations of the earth would be blessed. The seed of Abraham eventually leads to Jesus Christ, whereby every believer receives his inheritance by faith, and according to a spiritual circumcision (Colossians 2:11) that takes place through the acceptance of Christ. The covenant covers land provision, a bloodline of kings, a creation of nations, and the promise of God to in fact, be their God.

Prior to the coming of Christ, God's covenant with Abraham required that all males from Abraham's seed have a physical circumcision. Genesis 17:11 describes the circumcision as a token of the covenant; however, with the coming of Christ, there is now a circumcision of the *heart* that takes place. This is significant, because Jesus ushered in the beginning of a new covenant between God and mankind. The old covenant with Abraham required physical evidence to identify God's people." *And all the men of his house, born in the house, and bought with money of the stranger, were circumcised with him*" (Genesis 17:27). Today, we have but only to believe by *faith* that Jesus' finished work on the Cross has brought us into right-standing with the Father once again, repent of our sins, and accept Jesus as Lord. It is a process that takes place through sanctification, "because strait is the gate, and narrow is the way, which leadeth unto life, and few there be that find it" (Matthew 7:14).

IDENTIFYING WITH CHRIST

Once we have accepted Jesus as the Lord of our life, something miraculous takes place. It may not be noticeable at first, but there is a rebirth to a body that has just died! That's right, a spiritual rebirth. In order to receive Christ, we must die to *self*. In essence, it is a crucifixion of the flesh, (which is corrupt from birth, Genesis 6:12) giving way to the Holy Spirit; that He may indwell the believer, conforming the believer into the image of Christ.

Because of our inheritance through Christ, we become heirs to the Kingdom of God. We become subjects of a new headship and authority, partakers of a kingdom that shall have no end (Luke 1:33). Although we still have fleshly bodies, the very Spirit of God resides within us. Will we still continue to sin? Absolutely. Why? Because we are still experiencing the side effects of a sin nature that the body has had to deal with for a very long time.

Christ gives us a new nature. The Bible tells us that we are born of an incorruptible seed which shall live forever (1 Peter 1:23). Now, that's enough to shout about! You see, our actions no longer determine who we are, but rather where our *inheritance* lies. Once we fully grasp this concept, we can conquer so many obstacles that stifle our growth and limit our effectiveness for Christ. We must begin to act on the basis of our inheritance as opposed to the way that we feel. You may not *feel* like an heir to the kingdom, you may not *feel* that you've been born of incorruptible seed, you may not *feel* any different than you did the day before your conversion, but the Kingdom of God is not based on feelings, it's based on God's Word.

A GUIDING LIGHT

When visiting a foreign country or an unfamiliar place, there is always the possibility that you could wind up lost and in need of assistance to help you get back on track. This can be a frightening experience for some, especially if it's their first time in unfamiliar surroundings. The first, and most common reaction is to simply ask for directions. It is good to know that when we find ourselves in unfamiliar territory, we can always count on assistance from the Word of God. The Bible says, *"Thy word is a lamp unto my feet, and a light unto my path"* (Psalms 119:105). How comforting to know that in our times of darkness, when we've lost our way, the Word of God is like a beacon in the night, going yet before us that we may not lose our way.

The glorious light of the Word exposes hidden dangers along our paths that might otherwise bring harm to us. It helps us to navigate through the treacherous storms of life that can sometimes threaten to crush us under the mighty waves of despair and anguish. But the Word of God is a sustaining power; one that is unmatched by any force in the entire universe. It is by the same Word that the very foundations of the world were formed. What an awesome power to behold!

To have such an assurance in our time of need, when we're lost and can't find our way, the Word of God is our beacon, our illuminating force, to lead us ever forward in pursuit of the paths of righteousness.

THE COST OF UNBELIEF

There are several factors that can keep us locked into a "boxed in" environment. One of the primary factors is unbelief. We are conditioned from birth to believe only what we can see. We hear phrases like, "I'll believe it when I can see it," or "I can't believe what I just saw." One phrase requiring visual confirmation, the other is receiving the confirmation, yet *denying* the existence.

Such was the case during the time of Christ. Many required proof of His Deity, yet when it was demonstrated, some claimed His power was of "devils" (Matthew 12:24). Since the time of His crucifixion, although there were many eyewitnesses; there are those that still deny the crucifixion and resurrection of Christ. **Unbelief, through the ages, has robbed mankind of his inheritance; a purchase made by the precious blood that was shed upon the cross, in order to restore that which was lost so long ago. It is unbelief that limits our possibilities in Christ. It was Jesus, who said in Matthew 17:20, that if we have the faith as a grain of mustard seed, that we should be able to move mountains. Nothing should be impossible to us! Jesus was not talking of natural physical strength here, but supernatural power that could only be derived from our Heavenly Father.**

In His statement, He was pointing out the key that unlocks the realm of all possibilities, which is *faith*. According to Hebrews 11:1, "Faith is the substance of things hoped for, the evidence of things not seen." Faith and unbelief mix together like oil and water! One totally contradicts the other.

It is unbelief that keeps us from receiving God's best for our lives. When we are operating in unbelief, it is contrary to God's Word. Many Christians today are walking in defeat because of what they *don't* know concerning their inheritance. It's like meeting at the attorney's office for the reading of a will, and several family members fail to show up. In their absence, the will is read, but because they were not present to *hear* the reading, vital information is not communicated. Does this mean that the will is not valid? No, of course not. It simply means that whatever is contained in the will is of *non-effect* until all parties involved are contacted.

The contents of the will serve little purpose until released into the hands of the respective parties.

RECEIVING THE INHERITANCE

As heirs to the kingdom, believers inherit the promises of God. Just as some wills require that certain conditions be met in order to obtain the contents, so it is with the promises of God.

Certain conditions must be met in order to receive the promises. The first condition is *repentance*. Repentance is the turning away from sin. It is to reform one's way of living in order to bring about change. *Confession* is a condition that is essential as well. The act of confession forces the sinner to come to grips with his or her true state of being. It allows us to see just how we compare to a Most Holy and Most High God.

The next, and probably the most important step, is the *acceptance* of Christ as Savior. It is an absolute necessity to accept Jesus as Lord. Without Him, we can have no relationship with God, the Father. Jesus Himself said, "I am the way, the truth, and the life: no man cometh to the Father, but by me" (John 14:6). Once Christ is accepted, the Holy Spirit comes and takes up residence inside of the believer. It is at this point where the believer begins to experience the awesome change that takes place in their life. No longer is the believer guided by fleshly impulses, but rather he or she is led into the truth of God by His Spirit (John 16:13).

What a wonderful picture of the saving grace and mercy of God. He gives us His Holy Spirit to help navigate our way out of the confines of our "box." After the re-birthing process, we are called to water baptism (John 3:5). In John 3 v.3, Jesus stresses the importance of being "born again." He states that, "Except a man be born again, he cannot see the Kingdom of God."

You see, unless a spiritual rebirth takes place, the carnal mind *cannot* comprehend the things of God (Romans 8:6). He reveals Himself to us throughout Scripture. He illustrates His character, His nature, His mercy, goodness, and glory. If we are carnally minded, we totally misunderstand God and His purpose for our lives. It's like handing over a coach's playbook to someone who has never been introduced to the game. It just doesn't make sense!

THE WATER BAPTISM

As believers, we are called to be baptized as an outward showing of the death, or "putting away" of the "old" nature, and the "resurrection" of the new nature that we receive through Christ. *"Therefore if any man be in Christ, he is a new creature: old things are passed away; behold, all things are become new"* (2 Corinthians 5:17). The phrase, "to be born of water and of the Spirit," as stated in John 3 v. 5, has several interpretations. Jesus could have been making reference to the water baptism of John the Baptist, or perhaps using the word "water" to symbolize the Holy Spirit, according to *Nelson's Compact Bible Commentary*, authored by Earl Radmacher, Ron Allen and H. Wayne House. Water is referenced in actual physical birth, as well as being linked to the work of God.

RELATIONSHIP

In the context of a family, relationship is important. Even outside of the family, relationship is vital to our well-being. Man, from the very beginning was destined for relationship (Genesis 2:18). God Himself said, "It is not good for the man to be alone. I will make a helper who is just right for him" (NLT). God created the need for relationship. Without it, we can feel lost and disoriented. Those without relationship of some kind, often attempt to fill the void with other means. Unfortunately, the alternatives sometimes produce an unfruitful life.

Parents must have relationship with their children if they are to grow up in fullness and stature. The relationship of the parent to the child is vital to the impact on society. If a child is neglected or abused in relationship to the parent, then society is affected by the behavior the child may exhibit. On the other hand, if the relationship is one of nurturing and encouragement, the child in most cases, is productive and contributes well to society.

When we isolate ourselves, or become "lone rangers," we sometimes diminish our effectiveness. We need others in order to achieve God's best for us. The "lack" of relationship stunts our mental and spiritual growth. God's design for man is in every aspect, one that relates to family. Man was created in the image of God. Man has a physical body, which houses a soul and a spirit. He is a *three*-part being. God is a triune being, scripturally referred to in three Persons; God the Father, God the Son, and God the Holy Spirit.

Jesus, Himself provides clarity to the character and nature of God in John 14:9, when He explains to Philip that to see Him is to see the Father. Colossians 2:9 is further evidence that the fullness of the Godhead is found in Jesus. *"For in Him dwelleth all the fullness of the Godhead bodily."* In Genesis 1:26, God said, *"Let us make man in our image, after our likeness."* Who was the *"us"* that God was referring to? It was none other than the two other members of the Godhead; the *Son*, and the *Holy Spirit*.

Although the word "Trinity" is not found in the Bible, the Trinitarian doctrine is biblically based, as evidenced throughout Scripture. The first chapter of Genesis begins with, *"In the beginning God created the heaven and the earth."* John 1:1 speaks of the beginning referring to the Word. He says, "The Word was with God, and the Word was God. In the same chapter, verse ten states, "He was in the world, and the world was made by Him, and the world knew Him not." 1 Timothy 3:16 speaks of God being made manifest in the flesh. Jesus was indeed the Word of God, who became manifest in fleshly form. As clearly as the Trinitarian doctrine is described in Scripture, there are still those that find this concept hard to grasp. Some clearly reject the notion that one God exists in three Persons. Despite the evidence they say, "There is only *one* God," and that statement is one-hundred percent correct, however; let us not forget that *someone* was there with God in the beginning.

To better translate the Trinitarian concept, imagine a married man with children. Now, let's say that the man's mother lives in the same home as he and his family. To his children, he is a *father*, to his spouse, he is a *husband*, and to his mother, he is still yet a *son*. Is he still not the same man that was referred to in the beginning of this example? Of course, he is. He is the same person, only functioning in three separate capacities as far as *relationship* to his family. This is as close a comparison as can be made concerning God's relationship with us; each Person of the Trinity, operating in separate capacities, yet all functioning as one God. What an awesome God!

We, in our finite minds, cannot fully comprehend the depth of God, however; what we can comprehend is what He has revealed to us in Scripture. It is God's way of saying to us that He desires "relationship" with us. It is truly a remarkable thing when the Lord of Hosts, Creator of all things in heaven and earth, intervenes in time and world events, in the person of Jesus, to demonstrate His infinite love for His creation.

THE TRUTH SPEAKS OUT

How can skeptics continue to deny both the crucifixion and the resurrection of Christ when archeology itself confirms the claims of the Bible? Yes, it is true that artifacts and handwritten scrolls have been found (The Dead Sea Scrolls) that date back as far as 70 A.D. What's the significance of this? It means that because of the authenticity of the writings so soon after the crucifixion of Christ, the greater the possibility for actual eyewitness accounts of the event.

The Bible is the only book of its kind that not only makes claims through its Scriptures of people, places, and world events, but in many instances through science and archeology, has proven itself to be true. It is the only book of its kind that tells of future events, and up to this point in history, has been one-hundred percent accurate. That beats any book that has ever gone into print! The Bible has been the number one best-seller since the history of mankind, and the words written in it are *God-breathed*. That means that the words were written under the Divine inspiration of God. Because the words are inspired of God, they are inerrant and infallible.

Throughout the course of history, many attempts have been made to destroy the Bible, but such attempts have been futile. God Himself said, "Heaven and earth shall pass away, but My words shall not pass away" (Matt. 24:35). What a powerful statement! God is serving notice that nothing shall interfere with His Word, not only in time, but throughout all eternity!

Noted in the book, *When Skeptics Ask*, respected theologians Dr. Norman Geisler and Ron Brooks highlight the four arguments for the existence of God. They consist of the *moral argument*, for the existence of God, the *argument from design* of the universe, the *argument from creation*, and the *argument from being*. These four major categories are superbly argued in apologetic fashion, and most notably address the questions that most often confront the believer.

As the culture grows even more hostile toward the reality of absolute truth, it is a known fact that the Bible is not just another religious book, but in fact, an historical document. As mentioned earlier, its truths have been substantiated by actual eyewitness accounts of real events, and original writings that date back during the time of Jesus. Unlike other religious books, the Bible has within it the power to change lives.

Because the very heart of the Gospel centers on Jesus, it is no wonder that there is always controversy at the mention of His name. Because He *is* Truth, many reject Him. Because of the inherent sin nature within man, there is a natural rebellion to truth. Man, from the beginning of birth, is separated from God; from the aspect that he *cannot know God* until he accepts Christ.

Jesus said, "I am the way, the truth, and the life: no man cometh unto the Father, but by me." It is a very bold statement to say the least; but one that cannot be denied. Jesus is no stranger to controversy. His claims of Deity have sparked controversy amongst other religions for centuries; this despite the fact that historical data, as well as eyewitness accounts of His miraculous life support His claims. For instance, Jesus is the fulfillment of prophecy as told by the prophet Isaiah; the one who would be called Immanuel, "God with us." Isaiah elaborates in chapter 9 v. 6 when he says, "For unto us a son is given: and the government shall be upon his shoulder: and his name shall be called Wonderful, Counsellor, The mighty God, the everlasting Father, The Prince of Peace."

Jesus repeatedly accepted worship; an act reserved only for God. There were many who worshiped Him and confirmed His Deity. He is the agent by whom the world was created, as described in Colossians 1:16, and the disciples themselves recognized Him as God. In Colossians 2 v. 9,

Paul describes Jesus as being indwelt with the "fullness" of the Godhead. Thomas, after visually inspecting the wounds that Jesus received at crucifixion referred to Him as God. John 20 v. 28 reads, "And Thomas answered and said unto him, My Lord and my God."

Even after His resurrection, Jesus was sighted by more than five-hundred eyewitnesses, including His disciples, which further supports the claims of His Deity. "Verily, verily, I say unto you, before Abraham was, I Am," was the reply of Jesus in John 8 v. 58. The name "I Am," is the name by which God identified Himself to Moses in Exodus 3:14. God replied to Moses, "I Am That I Am: and he said, Thus shalt thou say unto the children of Israel, I Am hath sent me unto you."

So what, you may ask, is the reason for the explanations of who Jesus is? It is necessary to dispel the chaos that surrounds the name of Jesus. Understanding who He is, and why He came, is at the very core of the Gospel. The message is rejected by many because of a lack of understanding of His identity. To coincide with that is also the unwillingness to recognize and adhere to such a "moral standard" that has been "set" by God, in the form of *absolute truth*. Jesus is that Truth. In Matthew 10 v. 34 He says, "Think not that I am come to send peace on earth: I came not to send peace, but a sword." This verse has been grossly taken out of its context to imply something other than its original meaning. The inference here is that because there *is* such a thing as absolute truth, it is bound to create controversy because it sets a moral standard by which we should live. Jesus further elaborates in v. 36 in saying, "And a man's foes shall be they of his own household." Rebellion is sure to rise up in opposition to truth. If God's standards are being administered in the home, the initial response to those standards may be rejected. Why do you think children have a natural "bent" toward disobedience? It's because of the inherent sin nature that is derived from birth. We all have to be "taught" the truth of God. As that truth is accepted, then we are born of a new nature, one that is receptive to God's truth.

CREATIVE POWER

There is creative power in the Word of God. The first chapter of Genesis gives a vivid description of this creative power in the "spoken" Word of God. God merely spoke the world into existence. He had only to say, "Let there be," and it was! Now, that's power! The Word created an entire world from nothing, according to Hebrews 11:3. This is, of course contrary to those that believe in the "Big Bang theory" that all life sprang from an explosion somewhere in the galaxy, and earth somehow consists of matter that mysteriously came together to form our sphere. In actuality, it takes more faith to believe in such a theory than it takes to believe God at His Word!

One has but to only gaze into the heavens on a clear and star-filled night to witness the celestial splendor of intelligent design that could only have come from a Superior Being. If that's not enough, consider the awesome wonders that we enjoy here on the earth. The vast array of majestic mountains, deep blue seas, sprawling deserts, and yet tropical green rainforests, give testimony to a Creator. Each of these environments has a common interwoven thread. They all support some form of life, regardless of climate. Only an Intelligent Designer could orchestrate such a feat. God is not getting credit where credit is due. Man, in his arrogance, has attempted to discredit creation fact with his creation *fantasy.*

Once again, because of "unbelief" man has forced himself to the confines of the "box." By promoting theories, that in some instances have no scientific basis, man has attempted to silence God. Yes, that's right — silence God.

Man, as part of creation, has come to believe that *he* is the superior being in this universe; at least some would have us to believe. The deception is birthed through arrogance, which in turn breeds rebellion. When we rebel against God, we in essence are saying, "Leave me alone, I control my own destiny." Sometimes, God will give us what we ask for, usually leaving us to the consequences of rebellion. There are always consequences behind rebellion, because it is contradictory to the Word. The one action that is compatible with the Word is *obedience.*

Lucifer rebelled against God. He too is a created being who wanted to be like the Most High (Isaiah 14:14). Because of this insurrection he was cast down to the earth and destined for eternity in hell. Lucifer was arrogant and disobedient. Unfortunately, over the centuries he has manipulated mankind, through his deception, to follow his lead. The deception is by getting us to believe that there is no God, therefore man is free to exalt himself, and therefore in control of his own destiny. Wrong! That's exactly the attitude the enemy wants us to take. Because of his hatred for God, the Evil One has set himself against the things of God, especially man. Why? Because man has been created in God's image (Genesis 1:27). Satan has been forced over the centuries to live with the reality that he can never again be in fellowship with God.

Because we have been created in God's image, He has also given us a creative spirit. Over the centuries, man has exhibited wondrous creative abilities in architecture, sculptures, paintings, and craftsmanship, to name a few. Despite man's creative ability, it is important to note that it is all *God-given.* You see, God is the *author* of creation; therefore He is the only One that has creative power. However, God has given man the power to reproduce. So, what we see today in the form of art, skill, and talent is representative of our Creator.

FELLOWSHIP WITHIN THE BODY

For every Christian, fellowship within a local church body is absolutely essential. The Lord Himself thought it so important that He called us to do so in His Word. The Church is the means by which God teaches and blesses His people. It was Paul who said, "Faith cometh by hearing, and hearing by the Word of God" (Rom. 10:17). The Church is where the preaching of God's Word can be heard, therefore giving increase to the faith of the believer. The Church is God's representation of His heavenly kingdom. He has placed within the church, spiritual authority for the restraint of evil in this earthly realm. The Church is literally a conduit for the revelation of the Will and purposes of God.

Now, Christ is the Head of the Church. In fact, He gave His very life *for* the Church. Scripture refers to the Church as the bride of Christ (Rev. 21:9), who is presently awaiting the return of the bridegroom. Until then, the Church is to prepare itself for His return.

As members of the body, we are to encourage and pray for one another. Where there is unity, there is strength. In the days of the early church, the saints would come together during times of persecution in order to encourage one another. Today's circumstances dictate no less of a response from the Church. Christianity itself is under attack at a most unprecedented level. At no time since early church history, has the church been under such scrutiny. Why? Because it represents a standard. That standard is truth. You see, "God is truth" (John 14:6). He calls us to worship Him in spirit and in truth (John 4:24); the Spirit of truth guides us into all truth (John 16:13), and the knowledge of the truth shall make us free (John 8:32). Now, with all of this truth going around, is there any wonder why a fallen self-centered world persecutes the church? The problem is that absolute truth comes from God; the church is representative of that truth, and the truth of God demands *accountability*. The hearts of men are constantly seeking a release from that accountability by denying absolute truth.

It was in the context of persecution where the early church exhibited the awesome power for which it was established. In it and through it, by prayer, supplication, and obedience to Christ, when operating in the fullness of its godly authority; the early church was a beacon of hope in a world of darkness and chaos; a pillar of strength in times of spiritual weakness and despair, and a source of comfort in the midst of tragedy and grief. That same church is alive today, but it's up to the individual believer to utilize the authority that has been given by Christ.

MEMBERS OF THE BODY

As members of the body of Christ (because Christ is the Head of the church body), it would serve us well to remember that being part of a body comes with its responsibilities. Just as the human body has appendages, or *members*, so does the church body. Like the human body, each member is endowed with the ability to perform a certain function in relationship to the operation of that body. When a member does not function well, or perhaps severed from the human body, it impairs the function of the rest of the body. It hinders the ability of that body to operate at its peak efficiency level. Much the same can be said of the church body. If there is a member that does not function, or has been severed, the church cannot function at its full capacity. Each member is vitally important to the body in which it belongs. Jesus said, "I am the vine, ye are the branches: He that abideth in me, and I in him, the same bringeth forth much fruit: for without me ye can do nothing" (John 15:5). If a member is severed, for whatever the reason, Jesus says, that the severed member apart from him can do nothing. What a sobering thought.

The word "sever" means "to separate by, or as if by cutting," according to Webster. So when we as believers cut ourselves off from the church, we not only separate ourselves from our place of blessing, we hinder the blessings of others as well.

BLESSING OTHER MEMBERS

You are important to the body of Christ, because each member has been endowed with certain spiritual gifts. According to Scripture, these gifts are mighty for the tearing down of strongholds. When all members of the body are functioning in their capacity, one member aids in the function of another, just like the human body. If a certain member of the physical body is seized by a sickness or infirmity, then other members of that body work in conjunction in order to *purge* the infirmity. The body of Christ works in like manner. There are members in the church that are experiencing life's difficulties every day. At the same time, there are other members of that body that have already experienced perhaps, what another member is just beginning to face. Members of the body can benefit from saints that have already "gone through," and can get encouragement from someone who made it through.

A certain amount of maturity comes through trials; and when that maturity is exhibited for other members to witness, it can work wonders for a congregation. It allows those of lesser experience to witness the awesome power of God's glory at work in the life of a believer. In many cases, it allows one to get a first-hand look at the rewards for perseverance. By allowing God to use your circumstances in order to mature you as a believer, you in turn can be used in order to strengthen and edify the body. Isn't it awesome how God works!

TEARING DOWN THE TEMPLE

More than just a mere structure, the church is a representation of something much larger. Christ Himself demonstrated this in John 2:19 when He spoke of the destruction and "raising up" of the temple. But Jesus was not speaking of raising a physical structure; rather He was referring to the resurrection of the physical *body*. Because He had come to usher in a new covenant, the temple of God was no longer to be a structure built from man-made materials, but rather the Spirit of God was to take up residence in the individual believer. Christ is to live His life through us! That is precisely why the skeptics and Pharisees of His time branded Jesus as a heretic. He spoke in terms of the Spirit which they could not comprehend.

"Destroy this temple, and in three days I will raise it up" was the reply of Jesus in John 2:19. What was Jesus referring to? He was speaking from Kingdom principles. Jesus knew precisely why He had come, and for what purpose. He spoke from an *eternal* perspective, as His thoughts were constantly linked with the Father.

We, as a body of believers must learn to think and speak in terms of an eternal perspective. In order to do that we must do as Christ did, maintaining a constant relationship with God, the Father. The only way to that relationship is through Christ (John 14:6). It is then up to the Holy Spirit to guide us into all truth (John 16:13).

Today it is easy to lose sight of the words of John 2:19 as we are surrounded by churches of spectacular design and architecture. There is no shortage of man's creativity in the building of some of these structures. In our zeal to glorify God through our creativity, unfortunately sometimes we lose sight of the purpose of the church itself. The main purpose of the universal church is to evangelize, to equip the saints for service and proclaim the Kingdom of God. We have been commissioned by Christ to go into all the world to make disciples of men.

By and large, the church seems to be growing. As more of the culture searches for answers in our society, the increase in size and membership are good outward signs. However, let us not forget that the church (because of the new covenant) is now the individual *believer*. **Christ lives in us, and Christ is the Head of the church;** *we are the church.*

In these challenging times in which we live, the church can ill afford to take on the "box-like" mentality by confining itself to a structure, shutting out the rest of the world. We are called to be "salt and light" (Matt. 5:13-14) to a dying world: a preservative in this season of decay. The children of God are to set the standard through the preaching and teaching of His Word. We are not to be influenced by political correctness. Our marching orders come directly from Jesus. The church is to influence the culture, not to have the culture influence the church!

RADICAL CHANGE

All too often, we get caught up in "pop culture" marketing strategies to promote church growth. That's fine for bringing the masses in, but the question remains, where do we go from here?

The apostles were radical in their methods. They simply did as Jesus commanded and went "out" amongst the masses preaching and teaching the Word of God, healing the sick, (with the laying on of hands, Acts 8:17, Mark 5:23) and baptizing in the name of the Father, and of the Son, and of the Holy Ghost (Matt. 28:19). By taking this radical approach called "obedience," these men of God helped to change the course of human history. It's amazing what can happen through the simple act of obedience. God says in Malachi 3:6 that He doesn't change. He is the same yesterday, today, and forever. So why is it that the church feels that *it* must change? Granted, change is sometimes necessary concerning the method by which the culture is reached, however; the message of the Gospel must *never* be compromised. It is only through the Gospel that the culture can be influenced. Only through the Gospel, can lives be changed and healing take place. And it is only through the Gospel, can we as sinners, see ourselves for who we truly are, come to repentance and receive the salvation of the Lord, Jesus Christ. We receive this by faith, and the church plays a vital role in this process.

Therefore, it is imperative that the church is functioning at its full capacity. Certainly the times in which we live are desperate. The culture is searching for answers, and God has made provision for those answers through His Son, who is the Head of the church. This is no time for denominational debates concerning church doctrine; nor is there time for internal division within the church. So often we get caught up with "title" and positions of authority within the church, and we lose focus on the "big picture." This is just one of the deceptions of the enemy. The church must learn to recognize them when they occur, and deal with them accordingly. We can't afford to get caught up "in" the box, and lose sight of what's going on "outside" of the box. We need to wake up to what's happening to our culture, and "rise up" to meet the challenges as they are presented. God has not given us the spirit of fear; but one of power, of love, and of a sound mind (II Timothy 1:7). We have been given weapons, mighty for the tearing down of strongholds by Christ, Jesus (II Cor. 10:4)! It's time that we, as the church, use them with the authority that has been given to us by Christ. What would the apostle Paul think of the state of today's church? Do you think he would be prompted to write a few more letters concerning the lack of power within the church, or perhaps lack of understanding?

Confusion breeds *chaos*, and at the heart of chaos you will always find the enemy, the Evil One, whose sole intent is to disrupt, dispel, and destroy the things of God. The church stands in his way. What an awesome responsibility the church has! Despite the formidable methods of the adversary, when operating in all of its fullness, the church is more than capable of its task. It has all of heaven at its disposal! Jesus said, "Upon this rock I will build my church; and the gates of hell shall not prevail against it" (Matt. 16:18).

CHAPTER TWO

THE BIRTH OF CHAOS

"And he said unto them, I beheld Satan as lightning fall from heaven." (Luke 10:18)

The origin of chaos in human history can be traced back to the garden of Eden. This is, of course as we all know, where man succumbed to the temptations of the devil, thus introducing sin into the world. It is sin that promotes chaos. But to trace chaos to its root, we must first look to the heavens, venturing into eternity past, into the realm of angelic hosts; spirit beings created by God in order to serve His purpose. Angels, as we know them, were created not only to carry out the Will of God, but also to worship Him (Heb. 1:6). Long before the creation of man, there were angels. Throughout Scripture they have been used as messengers (Gen. 19:15, Matt. 24:31), as escorts (Luke 16:22), as warriors (Rev. 12:7), ministers (Mark 1:13), and administrators of God's justice (Rev. 9:15). In other words, angels aid in the administration of God's plan for humanity.

Much has been said from time to time about the possibility of other life forms in the universe. The proverbial quote, "We are not alone," although intended to refer to "extraterrestrial" beings (ET's or aliens), adequately expresses the reality of angels. Before the beginning of human history, there was God. He is an eternal and Supreme Being. He has *always* been and always *will* be. There was never a time when God was *not*. When God created angels, He also established a hierarchy amongst His angelic hosts. Just as an army by today's standards has its ranks of soldiers, so too does heaven's angels. The hierarchy is what's known as the archangels. They are placed in positions of authority over the other angels, somewhat like generals in comparison of ranking authority. They are commissioned by God to do His Will according to His purpose. Now, Lucifer was an archangel of great beauty, as described in Ezekiel 28:17. Because of his iniquity, he was cast down from the mountain of God. Vanity, pride, and arrogance were the badges of dishonor that Lucifer bore as he was cast down from grace.

THE ETERNAL BOND

What a terrible fate to be cast out of the presence of God. To suffer the anguish of separation from loved ones, at times can seem unbearable; but to be separated from the love of God is inconceivable for the believer. According to Romans 8 v. 35-39, neither tribulation, distress, persecution, famine, nakedness nor peril can separate us from Christ. How comforting it is to know that once we are in Christ that neither death, nor life, nor angels, principalities, powers, things present, nor things to come, nor height nor depth, nor any other creature, shall be able to separate us from the love of God. This is depth of love that he has for us.

THE TWO EDENS

According to Scripture, there was more than one garden of Eden; the earthly garden we have long since come to know as the first home of Adam and Eve. But the first

Eden was the one created in heaven known as *the garden of God*. This is the very garden described in Ezekiel 28 v. 13 that Lucifer was allowed to occupy. He was described as having been covered with every precious stone, including diamonds, sapphire, emerald and gold. He was anointed to sing as well, for Scripture also speaks of the workmanship of his *pipes*. But because of his vanity and pride, he was cast out of heaven and down to the earth. It was here inside the *second* Eden that he tempted man.

Think about it, Lucifer, a former archangel that has been cast down from the presence of God the Father only to exist in eternal separation and torment. If that wasn't enough, then came man, who was created a little *lower* than the angels (Psalms 8: 5-6), and was given dominion over the earth; and all things were put under his feet. The once elevated angel called "Lucifer" suddenly found himself being placed under the subjection of a lesser creature called "man."

DISORDERLY CONDUCT

"And there was war in heaven: Michael and his angels fought against the dragon; and the dragon fought and his angels, and prevailed not; neither was their place found any more in heaven." (Revelation 12:7-8)

The insurrection of Lucifer and his angels was costly. In his humiliation and defeat, he took along with him one-third of heaven's angels, as stated in Revelation 12 v. 4, and thus began his quest for control of the earth. Using this angelic rebellion as a back-drop, we can see the origin of chaos as it culminates in utter disobedience to the rule and authority of God.

A REBELLIOUS SPIRIT

The very meaning of the word "rebellion" is to resist authority, according to Webster. The Bible likens rebellion as unto "witchcraft" (1 Sam. 15:23). However it is perceived, God does not look favorably upon a rebellious spirit. When we rebel against those in authority over us, we remind God of Lucifer and his resistance to authority. The act of rebellion is rooted in pride and self-centeredness. When we take on the attitude that "It's all about me," we disregard the rule of authority, causing us to want to "go our own way," "do our own thing," the deception being that we know what's "best for us." Wrong! Only our Heavenly Father knows what's best for us, which is why we must seek His council in all matters, no matter how small. He desires to communicate with us on a daily basis. Christ came that we might have a relationship with Him.

God is not some cosmic dictator waiting to exterminate us if we make mistakes, or ask questions of Him. He wants us to know Him, which is why He gave us His inspired Word in order to reveal Himself to us. Because we can never fully comprehend God in the capacity of our finite minds, He relates to us according to our understanding. He gives us words like "father" and "mother" to assist us in the understanding of his nature. He illustrates this in the context of a family.

FAMILY TIES

The first family on earth was that of Adam and Eve. They were wed by none other than God Himself. According to Scripture, God caused a deep sleep to come upon Adam, and at that time He removed one of Adam's ribs (Genesis 2:21-22) and made a *woman*. When Adam saw her he stated in Genesis 2 v. 23 "This is now bone of my bones, and flesh of my flesh." Adam had just experienced the first surgical procedure ever performed, and God Himself was the doctor.

Now Adam, despite having gone through this ordeal, was conscious enough to realize what had just taken place. God in His wisdom and mercy saw that it was not good for man to be alone (Genesis 2:18), so with the creation of the woman, God made Adam *complete*. The woman was to complement Adam in every way: she was made to suit him.

Near the end of Genesis, chapter two, the woman is described as Adam's *wife*. This is significant because this clearly defines the meaning of "family." *"Therefore shall a man leave his father and his mother, and shall cleave unto his wife: and they shall be one flesh"* (Genesis 2:24).

It is a Covenant that God made with man in the very beginning, that he should procreate (multiply) and have dominion over the earth. Unfortunately, God's Covenant was broken, as chaos crept its way into the Garden.

CHAOS UNLEASHED

Prior to the crucifixion and resurrection of Christ, perhaps the most significant event in history was the *fall* of man. It marked the beginning of eternal separation from God and a rebellious allegiance with Satan. The reality of the statement is quite blunt, but in essence that is precisely what happened. You see, since God had given dominion of the earth over to man and the rule of the earth and everything in it was placed under man's foot, Satan was not only humiliated, but found himself also subjected to the rule of man. His only chance to once again reign over the earth was to convince man to relinquish his authority.

Once again, it all comes down to *authority*. When coupled with *dominion*, the two words form an awesome combination. Both authority and dominion originate with God. In His goodness and His mercy He relegated this incredible power to man, but the Tempter always comes to steal, kill, and destroy. God has given us authority over our circumstances today through our Lord Jesus Christ. He re-established the Covenantal promises of God concerning dominion and authority. The problem is that we get caught up focusing on the circumstances rather than the *promise*. In doing so we allow Satan to come in to *steal* our joy, *kill* our relationships, and *destroy* our families.

HATH GOD SAID?

Perhaps three of the most destructive words that have ever been spoken are *"Hath God said?"* This is the question that Satan posed to Eve in the Garden. The question was in regards to the now infamous "tree of the knowledge of good and evil." God had already made it clear to both the man and the woman that in the day that they chose to eat of that particular tree, that they would surely die (Genesis 3:3). Notice the phrase "chose to eat." In order for anyone to choose to do anything, signifies a "free will." We all have a free will; freedom to choose the paths we take in life. We can choose to accept God, or reject Him at our own risk, nevertheless; He gives us that freedom.

The enemy's strategy in the Garden was to plant *doubt* into the minds of the first newlyweds. Needless to say, he succeeded, and because of that the earth was cursed (Genesis 3:17-18). Adam was judged and God decreed that Adam would toil in the earth for all the days of his life in order to get the earth to yield food for him. Eve was judged, and consequently God deemed that she would suffer great pain during child birth, as well as having her husband rule over her (Genesis 3:16). A curse was placed upon the serpent as well, that he would crawl upon his belly and eat the dust of the ground for the rest of his days (Genesis 3:14).

The result of this rebellion is reflective of the world in which we live today. When a child is born into the world, the mother experiences a great deal of pain in the process of "labor." Once that child enters the world, he or she is entering a "cursed earth." Because the earth has been cursed, and the "first" parents having been judged, every child born after the first parents (Adam and Eve) is born with a sin nature; a propensity or desire to sin. In deceiving the man and the woman, Satan in effect caused them to view God through his eyes. In doing this, he somewhat persuaded them to go along with his plan, rather than the plan of God. This effectively gave dominion over the earth back to Satan.

The word "dominion" is derived from the word "domain." Webster describes domain as "complete and absolute ownership of land, a sphere of knowledge, influence, or activity." The Hebrew root word is *"radah,"* which means "to tread down, subjugate; prevail against, reign, rule." The world today is under the *influence* of Satan. When we view the world through the eyes of God, we can see the devastating effects of sin upon our culture. What we experience in today's world is directly related to the sin in the Garden, a break in the Covenant that was first established between God and man concerning dominion. Because of that break, sin was introduced into the world, chaos was unleashed, and man lost fellowship with God.

When we see and understand the residual effects of sin, it brings to mind a host of questions that long for answers. They are questions relevant to life that affect the quality of life. Questions that deal with poverty, sickness, disease, crime, violence, and war just to name a few, are on the minds of many today. But when we closely examine these issues, we should not despair. They only underscore our inadequacy to overcome the circumstances through conventional wisdom.

Proverbs 3 v. 5-6 instructs us to lean not to our own understanding, but in all our ways acknowledge God, and

He will direct our paths. Though we live in a "cursed earth," one that is filled with evil resulting from the "original sin" (from the Garden) is proof of our need for a Savior. It is the very reason why God sent His only begotten Son, that relationship between God and man would be restored, salvation would be made available, and the works of the enemy destroyed!

CHAPTER THREE

IDENTITY CRISIS

"He saith unto them, But whom say ye that I am? And Simon Peter answered and said, Thou art the Christ, the Son of the living God." (Matthew 16:15-16)

Does the phrase "identity crisis" ring a bell? Most of us are familiar with the term, possibly at some point and time, having gone through such a phase in life. It is somewhat common to experience this so called "identity crisis" during the adolescent years, mainly in transition from adolescence to adulthood. It can be difficult for many, but in the end, it amounts to only a phase of growth that most endure in a relatively reasonable amount of time.

Although adolescents struggle with identity, it is not limited to any particular age group. It may be more prevalent in some groups than others, but nevertheless it exists. The culture tends to identify with pop-icons in such areas as athletics, entertainment, industry and business, just to name a few. These icons most often live lifestyles that are equated with popularity and success, not to mention lavish and luxurious surroundings that exemplify the very pinnacle of earthly desires. Jesus was offered much the same after forty days of fasting and isolation in the wilderness, according to

Matthew chapter four. He was approached by Satan himself, in an attempt to take advantage of His perceived vulnerability. Having been without food for such a long period of time, Jesus' physical body was weakened, however; His spirit was strengthened. When confronted with the three temptations of the *world*, the *flesh* and the *devil*, the response came with the repetition of God's Word.

We live in the wake of constant attempts by the Tempter to lure us to the abandonment of God's Word. He knows that it contains power within it to accomplish God's Will for our lives. God said, "It shall not return unto me void, but it shall accomplish that which I please, and it shall prosper in the thing whereto I sent it" (Isaiah 55:11).

Just as Jesus resisted the onslaught of Satan, so too must we. That is one of the reasons why the study of Scripture is so important. We must study God's Word as II Timothy 2 v. 15 states, "Study to show ourselves approved, a workman that need not to be ashamed, rightfully dividing the word of truth." Why is this so important? Simply put, to destroy the works of the enemy, to compel him to flee! Jesus didn't panic, nor did He lose sight of His identity with the Father.

Jesus identified with God the Father because He was sent to do the Father's will. Mark 9 v. 37 illustrates the link between Jesus and God the Father. He said, "Whosoever shall receive me, receiveth not me, but Him that sent me." In other words, if you receive Jesus, then you are receiving the rule and authority of God over your life. In that particular verse, we see an illustration of the coming of the kingdom age. Our desires as believers should flow in line with that of Christ, to do the Father's will. Unfortunately, all too often we get distracted by the things of this world. Remember the temptations of Jesus; the world, the flesh, and the devil? These are the realities that we face on a daily basis. But Jesus overcame the temptations through *prayer*. He was in constant communication with God the Father, enabling Him to access unlimited power and authority. Prayer is the key when facing temptations.

When the world refers to a person's identity, it is usually defined by what a person does. In order to make a name for yourself you must achieve a certain goal or perform a certain task to be recognized. This is a deception of the enemy. The Christian's identity is linked to his or her birth (1 Peter 1:23). It is through the new birth that we are defined. Being born of an incorruptible seed, that seed being the Word of God. In fact, we are recognized as the *children* of God (Matt. 13:38). When we accept Jesus as Lord, the old nature is put to rest, dead to sin. In its place a new nature is formed, one that is born of God, a good and incorruptible seed that will never diminish. II Corinthians 4 v. 16 sums it all up in saying, "Though our outward man perish, yet the inward man is renewed day by day." The outward man perishes because he is dead to sin, his nature is of the flesh and the flesh is corruptible. Adam gives us this example in the Garden. But the inward man is of the Spirit of God. He is led by and feeds on the Word of God.

FILLING THE VOID

As we observe those around us who seek to find their identity through "materialism," there is evidence that there is a *void* that needs to be filled. We are a nation of mass consumers. We accumulate "stuff" in order to fill the void. Matthew 6 v. 20 speaks to this obsession by telling us to invest in the treasures of heaven rather than earthly riches, where everything is susceptible to perishing. There are people that feel that they have to buy a new automobile every two years for fear of falling out of step with the latest model. Worldly thinking have some convinced that they are better recognized and more readily accepted based on the car that they drive. It becomes a "status symbol" of achievement. There's nothing wrong with owning a nice automobile, but when the material possession becomes the gauge from which the person identifies him or herself, chaos develops. The possession then has the potential of becoming an *idol*. An idol is anything that comes between you and your relationship with the Living God. We must always be on guard against idolatry. What about the person who can't afford that new automobile or can't afford any means of transportation? Does that make them less of a person? Of course not! And that is precisely why your identity should not be tied to material possessions.

So many of our youth are bombarded with materialistic ads in the media. Many, if not most of these ads, are profit oriented that cater mainly to the desires of the flesh. Just a couple of years ago, many of the clothing stores carried lines of clothing for young ladies that were "questionable" to say the least. As with all generations, fads come and go and this particular fad was no different. The idea that women were not only purchasing, but wearing clothing supposedly designed for "outerwear," came just shy of the equivalent of "underwear" that should have never been sanctioned for public viewing; at least not while *on* the person. To top it all off, there were many Christian parents that bought into the "fad," allowing their moral standards to be lowered to those of the world. The apostle Paul tells us in Romans 12 v. 2 not to be conformed to this world but to be *transformed* by the renewing of our minds, that we may prove what is good and acceptable and the perfect will of God.

What is it that causes irrational thinking, eventually resulting in moral dilemmas? The answer lies in the void that is left unchecked, a spiritual hole that can only find its fulfillment in a personal relationship with the Lord Jesus Christ. When there is an absence of Christ in someone's life, there is also an absence of identity. At no time can a *spiritual* problem be satisfied with a worldly remedy. This is what is happening with some of our youth, as well as adults; trying to resolve spiritual issues through worldly means.

For most who are in search of an identity, there is an overwhelming desire to connect with something or someone for acceptance. In the example of the indecent clothing, the need to identify with a particular person happened to be the motivating factor. At the time, there was a famous pop-icon who frequently paraded around on the stage in scantily clad attire as part of an "act." Rock stars, movie stars, athletes etc. all have one thing in common; they entertain. That's what they do, that's part of their industry, and they do it well. The problem is that because they are in the spotlight, they are viewed as "idols." We pay attention to what they wear, who they date, how they style their hair, what their diet consists of, and the list goes on. We try vainly to imitate them in every possible way in the hope of possibly identifying with their celebrity status. But this is all *vanity*, and vanity according to the Bible is the equivalent of a lie or *deception*. The Greek translation of the word *mataios*, means empty, profitless, vain, idol.

From children to adults, clothing lines are adorned with the names of everyone's favorite athlete or celebrity. The owners delightfully advertise for all to see the "latest" in his or her particular line of apparel. Again, there's nothing wrong with having nice things, but the world offers us "material" things to identify with. The sad reality is that there are so many of our youth that live near or close to poverty levels, yet their focus is stayed on insignificant "status" symbols, namely extremely over-priced clothing that defies the imagination! In many instances some kids are willing to go to whatever lengths necessary to attain clothing, that no more identifies the person than the name that is stamped on the clothing itself! "Chaos" develops because a void is left unchecked. Some teens are moved to violence against one another in an attempt to attain what they believe to be a symbol of "status," a means of "identity," all because the void has not been filled. While situations like this are happening all over the country, Satan is reveling in his perversions upon our youth! Because they represent the next generation, the future recipients of the blessings of Abraham, they have been targeted by the Tempter. His sights are focused upon them, and he's been having a field day!

Our children are being held captive by the decadent and idolatrous grip of "materialism," and entangled in a web of deception designed to alter the plan and the purposes of God. From body piercing, to outrageous "tats" (tattoos), we witness outward manifestations of spiritual turmoil within. The need to *identify* creates an insatiable hunger of the heart that cries out for fulfillment. The void *must* be filled, the hunger satisfied. We, as Christians, must seize every opportunity to dispense God's truth. We are called to be "salt and light" to a decaying world. The voids *will* be filled one way or another. If we are "passive" and neglect our call to the Great Commission, surely darkness awaits to fill the void, however; if we exercise love, patience, and obedience to an Almighty God, we could be used to point the way to the only *true* fulfillment of the heart, the Lord Jesus Christ!

BLOODLINES

Just as we are born into an earthly family, we carry the name of our earthly parents. Even if we decided to change the birth name, we cannot alter the blood that flows through the body. The "blood" plays a vital part in who we are. God thought the blood to be so important, that He gave illustrations of its importance throughout Scripture. From the Edenic Covenant (God's first covenant with man) to the Everlasting Covenant (the eternal covenant) God reveals man's ties to "the blood."

In Genesis 4 v. 10, God spoke of the voice of Abel's blood crying out after he had been slain by his brother Cain. All throughout the Pentateuch, (the first five books of Moses) the blood of animals was used to sprinkle on the altars of sacrifice. In Old Testament law, if the innocent blood of man was shed, God required that the perpetrator be put to death. In the New Testament, Matthew 16 v. 17, Jesus speaks to Peter in reference to His identity replying to Peter, "Blessed art thou, Simon Barjona; for flesh and blood hath not revealed it unto thee, but my Father which is in heaven."

Why is "blood" mentioned in the Bible all the way through from Genesis to Revelation? And what does the blood represent? The blood represents "life." It is what Christ shed for us that we who were "dead" in our sins might live. From the very beginning in Genesis, God Himself killed the first animal, in order to cover Adam and Eve with skins after their sin against Him. What's the significance? Not only was it a precursor to the Atonement of Christ on the Cross, but God was showing in this illustration that the shedding of blood was *necessary* for the remission of sin. Hebrews 9 v. 22 speaks to this in saying, "And almost all things are by the law purged with blood; and without shedding of blood is no remission." Not only was the shedding of blood necessary, but God *required* it (Ezekiel 33:8).

Through our veins flows the bloodline of our ancestors from one generation to the next, carrying the genetic code of our earthly identity. Our DNA code links us to our parents at birth, becoming genetically "locked" to our birth parents for life. The blood tells the true story. It becomes our "life source" of identity. In Christ, the blood that He shed on Calvary is our means of identity. Because it covers our sins, we are drawn closer to God the Father (Ephesians 1:7). The DNA that signifies our link by way of the blood is the Holy Spirit. He is our "Identifier," our "Seal of approval" of righteousness. His task is to preserve us until the day of

Christ's return (Ephesians 4:30). He is also referred to as the "Comforter," the One who leads and guides us to all truth (John 15:26).

You cannot separate God from truth. They are both one and the same. Jesus proclaims that He is the way, the *truth*, and the life and that *no* man comes to the Father but by *Him* in John 14 v. 6. With Jesus being *truth*, the Holy Spirit leading us *into* truth, and God the Father never separating *from* His truth, the members of the Godhead are inexorably linked. As believers, we are linked to Christ by the blood, sealed by the Holy Spirit, and according to Ephesians 2 v. 6 have been raised *with* Christ and seated in heavenly places.

IDENTITY THEFT

Familiar with the term "identity theft?" Most of us are, in this information age. A person's "life packet" of information can be bought and sold for little or nothing in this world of high-tech. Doesn't that make the hairs on the back of your neck stand on end? It should! It happens to be one of the biggest problems in our culture today. Although its popularity as the most significant problem of our time is debatable, it certainly runs high on the list of major concerns. And rightfully so, after all, a person's identity is the only means by which others can determine who that person really is. In other words, your identity is your "passport" to *relationship*. For instance, let's say you walk into a bank with a check made out to you in your name, but you forgot your wallet or purse, which contains your picture ID. Let's assume you were in a hurry to rush to the bank in order to get there before closing time. You're new in town, and haven't had a chance to set up an account at a local branch. Chances are the teller will reject your attempt to cash the check based on your inability to produce some form of identity, a means by which the bank can determine who you are. At that moment, any potential relationship between you and the bank becomes distant due to lack of identification. Any attempts to withdraw funds from the bank are put on hold pending verification of identification.

Because of the Holy Spirit, we are recognized by God the Father as "righteous." He considers us as righteous, not by our own "works," but because of our acceptance of His Son, Jesus. Paul speaks of David in Romans 4 v. 6 as he describes how blessed the man is whom God imputes righteousness without works. By accepting Christ, we are adopted into the Kingdom of God (Romans 8:15), sealed with the Holy Spirit (Ephesians 1:13), and become heirs to God through Christ (Romans 4:7). As an heir to God the Father through the Son, we have *access* to the kingdom. Our relationship to the Father is made possible by way of the "blood." Because of Christ's death on the Cross, His blood having been the propitiation for sin, breaking both the power of sin and having paid the penalty for sin, we have been set free! We no longer have to live under the condemnation that sin brings. Because He has conquered death and sin by way of the Cross, He also has given us a means of escape.

When God looks upon those who have accepted His Son, He no longer sees the sin; instead He only sees the "covering," the cloak of righteousness that only the blood of the Lamb can bring. So, when we, children of the living God (because we are heirs to God, Romans 4:7), are in need, no matter what the circumstance, we can go to our Heavenly Father because we now have access because of our "bloodline." We are identified because of the seal of the Holy Spirit.

Let's use another illustration. Let's say again, that you are a stranger in a new town. This time, you are running late for work, the first day of your new job and you forgot to grab your purse (or wallet) before leaving home. Your I.D. is left inside as you rush to get to your car. In your haste, you inadvertently run through a red light, consequently drawing the undivided attention of a nearby police officer. He pulls you over, and the first thing he asks you for is your license and registration. He wants to know by what *authority* you have to operate the vehicle. You reach in your pocket to produce the identification, only to find that it's not there. You open the glove compartment, frantically searching, only to come up empty. Suddenly, you remember where you left it, only now, any attempts at explanation are futile. In the officer's eyes you are already *suspect* because of your failure to produce a form of identity. You now stand the risk of being arrested, and or possibly incarcerated for breaking the law. Any potential positive relationship you could have had regarding the law is now in jeopardy pending verification of identification. Until that time, you are placed in "handcuffs," consequently *restricting* your freedom. You suddenly find yourself placed in a form of *bondage*, all because of your inability to prove who you are.

In Christ we have a passport to relationship with the Father. Because of the "bloodline," we are not restricted by the "curse" of the law, which is the law of "sin and death." Because of Christ those who believe are now under the authority of the law of the "Spirit of life in Christ Jesus" (Romans 8:2). The problem for many is that they continue to operate according to the "old" law of sin and death. Jesus came that we may have *life* and have it more abundantly, according to John 10 v. 10. Because of who we are in Him, we are privy to all of the rights and privileges established by Christ through His resurrection. It is through His resurrection that Christ established the law of the Spirit of life. It is in fact a higher law that supersedes the old law of sin and death. The law of the Spirit of life releases us from the bondage of sin giving us the freedom to operate in the authority given to us by Christ as an heir to the Kingdom of God. The apostle Paul was so convinced of the love of Christ for us, in Romans 8 v. 38-39 he stated, "For I am persuaded, that neither death, nor life, nor angels nor principalities, nor powers, nor things present, nor things to come, nor height, nor depth, nor any creature, shall be able to separate us from the love of God, which is in Christ Jesus our Lord."

What a sobering thought. There is absolutely nothing either in heaven or earth that can separate us from the love of God. So when feelings of guilt of a particular sin infiltrate our thoughts, know that for the believer, Christ has covered a multitude of sins. We can confess our sins before the Father, and because of Christ, He will be faithful and just to forgive us our sins, and to cleanse us from all unrighteousness (1 John 1:9).

The problem with most of us is that we allow the circumstances to dictate the outcome of a particular situation. We must exercise the authority we have been given in Christ to overcome our situations. We must look beyond the *visible* and focus on the *invisible*. Colossians 1 v. 16 speaks of Christ as Creator of *all* things in heaven and in earth, visible and invisible, whether they be thrones, or dominions, or principalities, or powers. It goes further by stating that all things were created *by* Him and *for* Him. That pretty much says it all! Christ has been given authority over all things. There is nothing that He does not have authority over.

Now, if we know that God's Word is infallible and inerrant, and knowing that because of the character and nature of God, He is incapable of a lie (because God is truth, John 15:26), why do we as believers continue to allow Satan to steal our identity? According to Scripture, we are more than conquerors (Romans 8:37), we have been given weapons mighty for the tearing down of strongholds (2 Corinthians 10:4), and of a chosen generation, a royal priesthood (1 Peter 2:9). These are truths the enemy doesn't want you to know. For some, simply knowing the truth is alright, as long as the truth is not put into "practice." James 1 v. 22 exhorts us to be not only "hearers" of the Word, but also "doers" of the

Word. You see, it's the faith that's coupled with the Word, along with our testimony, that enables us to overcome the enemy's deception.

In Matthew 16 v. 13, Jesus asked the disciples "Whom do men say that I the Son of man am?" They replied in v. 14 saying, "Some say that thou art John the Baptist: some, Elias, and others, Jeremias, or one of the prophets. In v. 16 Peter answered, "Thou art the Christ, the Son of the living God." Jesus replied by saying, "Blessed art thou, Simon Barjona: for flesh and blood hath not revealed it unto thee, but my Father which is in heaven." It was the Spirit of God that revealed Jesus' identity to Peter; and by faith he received the confirmation. Our faith plays a huge role in receiving our identity. You first have to believe that Christ died on the Cross for the remission of sin, then resurrected by the power of the Holy Spirit, and all power in heaven and earth has been given to Him by God the Father. When we take God at His Word and begin to act on what He says in it, then can we experience the power of miracles in our lives, just as the apostles witnessed while walking with Jesus. As they began to identify with Him, the limitations they once knew prior to His coming were melted away as their faith and knowledge of the Son of God increased. Why is that? Because they began to "do" as He commanded. Even now, as we are faced with adversities, as we practice the application of God's Word, *change* takes place. Isaiah 57 v. 13 says when we put our trust in God, we shall possess the land and inherit His holy mountain! How many times are we faced with adversity, and listen to what the enemy has to say? Some will probably say, "I don't listen to the enemy, I listen only to God!" The reality is that you're *listening* to both; the question is, which are you responding to? If you, as a believer are responding to your circumstances based on fear or emotion, then you are most likely responding to the enemy. However, if you are responding to circumstances based on what God says, then you are responding to God's Word. The response comes in knowing who you are in Christ. That's what makes all the difference.

When you know that "Greater is He that is in you than he who is in the world" (1 John 4:4), you can face adversity with a different mindset. No longer are the artificial trappings of the world necessary to establish our identity. We don't have to hide behind trendy fads that come and go or even the pursuit of vanity or wealth. The truth is in order to enter the Kingdom of God, your I.D. will be required. Only those with a birth certificate stamped, "born of the incorruptible seed," will be allowed to enter. It will be those who are born of God, who come by the way of the "blood" of Christ and "sealed" by the Holy Spirit!

CHAPTER FOUR

CHAOS AND THE PRODIGAL SON

"Hear, O heavens, and give ear, O earth: for the Lord hath spoken, I have nourished and brought up children, and they have rebelled against me." (Isaiah 1:2)

Perhaps one of the most debilitating circumstances any parent can face, outside of the physical loss of a child, is coming to the realization of losing control of a son or daughter. Losing control, not in the sense of "authority," but rather control in the sphere of "influence." The loss of such influence can be difficult, to say the least. At times, it can be down right gut-wrenching and heartbreaking, especially for the parent who seeks to raise their child in the fear and admonition of the Lord.

There is no greater example of a parent's love and anguish than that of our Lord. As our Heavenly Father, He cares for us, and wants only the best for us (1 Peter 5:7). God demonstrated His love for Israel constantly, yet at every opportunity, there was rebellion and disobedience. After having been taken out of the land of Egypt, having endured over four hundred years of slavery, God's people showed their appreciation by wanting to return to the land of their masters (Exodus 16:13). How difficult this must have been; God, our Heavenly Father, who gave so much of Himself for the welfare of His children only to see them turn away from Him in disobedience.

As a parent, there will be times when you give your all for the well-being of your child, and appreciation may be slow in coming, if at all. But regardless of appreciation, we as parents are responsible for their upbringing. We have been placed as stewards over their lives in order to teach them and raise them up according to God's statutes. The road is not often easy, and the paths are sometimes dark. But as stewards over His children, we as parents must learn to depend on the light of His Word to help us to navigate.

A FATHER'S LOVE

There is no love that can compare with the love that our Heavenly Father has for us. He gave His only begotten Son that whosoever believes on him would not perish, but have everlasting life, according to John 3 v. 16. This kind of love is what's known as *agape* love. The Greek term, according to Webster, means unselfish, unconditional love for another. This is the kind of love that Jesus exhorts us to have for one another. Speaking as a parent, and father of a son, I cannot even begin to comprehend the depth of love that caused God the Father, to allow His only begotten, to be nailed to a cross for the sake of "my" sins. What tremendous love it must have been, to cause the second member of the Godhead (who is Christ) to leave His exalted position in heaven and come to earth in bodily form, and offer to us salvation. Such love, the world has never known!

Luke, chapter 15 gives a vibrant illustration of a father's love for his son in Jesus' parable of the prodigal. In his haste to receive his inheritance, the son in the illustration approaches his father and asks for that portion that has been set aside for him. He goes away, into what the Bible describes as a "far country," and squanders the inheritance in riotous living. As a result, he finds himself destitute, at one point eating the leftovers of pigs. Eventually, he comes to his senses; realizing the goodness of his father, he returns to him in repentance and utter humility. His father, rather than revile his son, chose instead to receive him with open arms of acceptance back into the family. In doing so, restoring all that had been lost in riotous living, and demonstrated the agape love that is purely unconditional. The parable of the "prodigal" is God's illustration to us of His unconditional love. At times, we have wandered off into a "far country," after receiving God's blessings, only to squander our inheritance on riotous living.

THE VALLEY OF THE "SHADOW"

Just prior to our children's entrance to the teen years, I can recall having a conversation with my father-in-law regarding this most anticipated period of challenge. I refer to it as such simply because it is a time of significant change; despite all attempts of preparation. It can be a period when you are taken out of your "comfort zone," catapulted out of the "box," and are drawn ever closer to God. In our conversation, he delightfully chuckled, as if to say "You have no idea of what you are about to face!" He compared the experience to "Walking through the valley of the shadow of death." Now granted, this analogy may seem a little extreme, but eventually I began to see what was meant by his comment.

You see, the Psalmist in Psalms 23 likened "the valley of the shadow of death" to a time of "darkness" or "despair" in one's life. It signifies looming or impending danger that comes to hurt or destroy. He goes on the say in v. 4 that he would fear no evil, for God is with him. He continues in saying "Thy rod and thy staff, they comfort me." It is interesting to note that Psalms 23 is an illustration of the Good Shepherd as He watches and cares for the sheep. The "rod," as used by most shepherds in the conventional sense, is used for reproof or *"correction."* The rod in the context of the psalm however; refers to God's Word.

According to II Timothy 3 v. 16, "All Scripture is given by inspiration of God, and is profitable for doctrine, for reproof, for correction, for instruction in righteousness." The "staff" in the context of the psalm, is a metaphor for the work of the Holy Spirit. A shepherd guides the sheep by the use of his staff. Whenever they tend to stray away from the flock, it is the *staff* that is used to guide them back to safety. That is what the Holy Spirit does to us, who are His sheep. The Spirit guides us into all truth, the truth being Jesus; because He is the way, the truth and the life!

My introduction to the "valley" took place some five years ago, after the death of my father. It was a difficult time for our family, particularly for our children as they had just entered their teens. They were just in the initial phase of their "identity crisis," and then came the reality of the death of their grandfather. Needless to say, there were many sleepless nights from which they wrestled with their emotions, pondered God's sovereignty, and struggled with such a deep sense of loss. At the time, neither of our children had been firmly rooted or grounded in the Word. Consequently, in the months following my dad's death, chaos began to envelope our home. I had just begun my studies in a local Bible College when the "evil day" came calling on our household. Paul mentions this evil day in Ephesians 6 v. 13. He exhorts us to put on the whole armor of God that we might be able to *stand* when such a day arrives. The evil day, in this instance, found me ill-prepared, unaware of the tumultuous sea of adversity that was soon to follow. I didn't realize it at the time, but

I had already begun my descent into the valley. Although having been grounded in the Word myself, I was still in the process of grieving. The word "grief," is literally defined as emotional distress caused by bereavement. My heart was in a state of anguish and the thought of "separation" from my father gave birth to that grief. As I reflect on that time, I am reminded of separation from our Heavenly Father. Should we not experience that same anguish and grief when we, as Christians are separated from Him?

It was during my valley experience that I witnessed the power of God on a personal level. It was there that I learned how to trust Him in every circumstance, every situation. It was there where I learned to yield to His wisdom, His guidance, His awesome strength in my weakest moments. It was there in the valley of the "shadow" of death that I learned to relinquish control, submit to the authority of Christ, and allow myself to be enveloped in the purpose and will of God. In the valley, there is darkness. Sometimes you can't see where you're going, every footstep is a journey into uncertainty, every breath taken, a gasp for relief. The trails are winding and wicked, and at every crossroads, every juncture, there comes yet a still small voice that says, "Trust me." If you've heard it, then perhaps you *too* have been through the valley. Perhaps you are still in it. If so, remember that God's Word is a lamp unto your feet and a light unto your path (Psalms 119:105).

Isaiah 40 v. 4 proclaims that, "Every valley shall be exalted, and every mountain and hill shall be made low: and the crooked shall be made straight, and the rough places plain." So you see, no matter how low, no matter how dark or crooked the paths in the valley may get, know that the Good shepherd is nearby. He is there to guide you by His Word, but you must have an ear to listen...to the yet still small voice.

THE PROWLING LION

As a parent, you always want what's best for your child. From birth, you plan for their future as a good parent should do. But what do you do when your plans seem to go up in smoke? What takes place when that child begins to exercise the free will that God has placed inside of them? For many parents, it can be the beginning of a nightmare. For some, it becomes a "valley" experience. Such was the case in my own personal experience. As I stated earlier, the chaos began shortly after the death of my father, and rapidly progressed thereafter. I remember one evening talking with my son over the phone, asking him about school. I was at work at the time, but I could detect a kind of "distance" in his voice. He didn't seem to be fully engaged in the conversation, as if to be hiding something. So, I asked him "Is anything wrong?" He replied, "No dad, nothing's wrong." I could tell that he wasn't himself. His grades had been slipping in school, and I had been getting reports from teachers about the company he had been keeping. While I was concerned about all of these things, I was also mindful that he was still grieving over the loss of his grandfather. Nevertheless, I reminded him that his grandfather would have wanted him to succeed and do well in school. Despite my best efforts, he seemed to slowly drift away from me.

I can recall one evening in another phone conversation with him, talking about a situation that had developed with one of the neighborhood bullies. Again, I was at work and regretted that I could not be there to talk this particular situation over with him face to face. He was only thirteen at the time, and the bully in question was seventeen. The neighborhood bully had tormented my son for weeks without my knowledge, and it had finally come to a showdown. My son called me for advice as to what action to take. Apparently, the bully had come to pay a visit in our own front yard, knowing that I was not at home. I pondered over my responsibilities as a father, a provider and protector of our home. I was also aware of God's Word concerning the temptations of the enemy. In this case, the enemy was appealing to my son's *pride*. As I continued to speak with him, I had to come to a decision, quickly, decisively. I regret that my decision was carnally based, rather than that of godly wisdom. I allowed myself to get caught up in a *worldly* response to a *spiritual* situation.

The bully was on the prowl, as a lion, seeking whom he may devour! My son became his prey. He was young, weak, not just concerning his age in comparison to the older boy; but because of his infancy in the Word. You see, because God's Word is powerful, had I properly instructed my son in the ways of righteousness, the odds against him that evening would have been substantially diminished. He sought counsel from me, his dad, before taking action. As I reflect on that evening, it was a reminder to me as to what I should have done to guide me in my decision-making. We should always seek the counsel of our Heavenly Father when faced with decisions. Job 12 v. 13 proclaims, "With Him is wisdom and strength, he hath counsel and understanding." Regrettably, the counsel that was given to my son was of a carnal nature. I allowed myself to be seduced by pride, and the result proved to be disastrous. After the chaos erupted, and the inevitable fight between the two boys ensued, my son called me again, stating that it was over. He had successfully defended his pride, but nevertheless; the battle had been lost. He wasn't visibly hurt on the outside, but on the inside was the possibility of spiritual damage, which became my greatest concern. The Bible teaches us to "love thy neighbor as thyself." It's not a suggestion, it's a commandment! I failed at teaching my son this Biblical principle. I failed, because I was caught up in pride, and pride isolates you from God.

When you are isolated from God, you become prey for the enemy, who is *always* prowling as a roaring lion...seeking whom he may devour. That evening, the Destroyer was able to get two for the price of one. Had we both dressed up in the *full* armor of God that day, the outcome may have been quite different. The enemy is *constantly* searching for cracks in your armor. If he can't find a crack in yours, he will attempt to find one in someone who is close to you. Ephesians 6 v. 11 instructs us to "put on the whole armor of God that we might be able to stand against the wiles of the devil." If you are not properly suited for battle, the enemy will have his way. That is why it is imperative that parents pray for their children. Just as it is an obligation of the parent to dress their child when they are too young to dress themselves, so too should that parent have the same obligation in dressing their "spiritual" infant; which can be done through prayer.

The thief comes in the darkness, in order to kill, steal and destroy. He is no respecter of persons — his target... anyone who is unprepared, separated from the flock, void of wisdom and the knowledge of God. "But we have been given weapons mighty through God, for the tearing down of strongholds," proclaims II Corinthians 10 v.4. One of the most potent weapons in that arsenal is prayer.

I had been given another chance, a chance to "get it right" with my son. That had become a primary concern of my father before his passing. I was away from home frequently because of work commitments. Constantly, I was reminded by my dad that I needed to spend more time at home, especially during the teen years. Prior to that time, I had very little grasp on Philippians 4 v. 19, where it states that "God shall supply all of my needs according to His riches in glory by Christ Jesus." The deception was in thinking that I was to supply all of my family's needs. In doing so, I began to work longer hours, which left my family vulnerable to the schemes of the Tempter. I had read over Philippians 4 v. 19

before, but had never really *meditated* on it. When you meditate on something, it becomes a part of you. As it is put into practice, change comes about. Despite my best effort, the Evil One was relentless. Not long after the first incident, the floodgates seemed to burst open. I received a call from the vice principal of my son's school one day, concerning his conduct. He had been held in detention for cutting classes, and during detention asked to be excused for a restroom break. Needless to say, he never returned to class. I left work and arrived at the school in record time, only to find him in a rather obscure area outside of the school building; apparently hiding with another student. His behavior was beginning to change. His innocence was beginning to wane. "This isn't the son that I had raised," I thought. His actions were now becoming contradictory to his upbringing. What was taking place was the beginning of a battle for his soul. The Word that had been planted in him since his birth was now in danger of being taken away. Mark 4 v. 15 speaks of Satan coming immediately to take away the Word that is sown in the heart. As both my son and I were enthralled in the pain of grief, I neglected to see the gathering storm in the early stages of chaos; a storm of immense proportions.

THE STORM INTENSIFIES

When you're in the midst of a storm, it gets difficult at times to stay focused on God. The disciples are prime examples of this in Matthew 8 v. 25. They feared for their very lives when the waves of the sea threatened to overtake their ship. But in verse 26, Jesus is awakened from His sleep and rebuked the waves and the sea became calm again. Before His rebuke of the waves, He proclaimed, "Why are ye fearful, O ye of little faith?" There are two key words in His response. They are "fearful" and "faith." If you are fearful of your circumstance, there is no room left for faith. On the other hand, if you have faith, even the size of a mustard seed, you can move mountains.

In the weeks that followed my son's downward spiral, I began to experience feelings of guilt. I began to have thoughts that questioned my judgment as a parent, thoughts that caused me to temporarily live under the umbrella of self-condemnation. They were fiery darts hurled by the enemy. But as I began to meditate on Scripture, I realized that there is no condemnation for those who are in Christ Jesus, who walk not after the flesh, but after the Spirit (Romans 8:1). As I began to walk more in line with the Word of God, I sensed the storms surrounding me gathering intensity. From one chaotic episode to the next, it seemed that I was being bombarded with a deluge of trials that demanded all of my attention. I was reminded of I Peter 4 v. 12 that states, "Beloved, think it not strange concerning the fiery trial which is to *try* you, as though some strange thing happened to you." Although I was aware of the truth of God, there were times when I failed to *practice* it. The truth of the matter is I was operating in disobedience. It was James who said, in chapter 1 v. 22, "But be ye doers of the word, and not hearers only, deceiving your own selves." There were many times that I deceived myself, thinking that I could handle the problems that seemed to crop up overnight. By now, my son had just turned fifteen. The calls from school continued with such frequency, that eventually he was suspended. How could this be happening? What was I doing wrong? These are common questions asked by many parents of prodigals. There is a point where it seems that no amount of discipline seems to get through. I had reached that point with my son. He did not seem to respond to any conventional methods of discipline.

In retrospect, I realize the reason was because of my failure to use God's principles for instruction. Instead, I used worldly wisdom, which I Corinthians 3 v. 19 proclaims is "foolishness" to God. All too often, I took matters into my own hands, feeling that his rebellion was against me, when it really wasn't. I was wrestling not against flesh and blood, but against principalities and powers, against the rulers of the darkness of this world, against spiritual wickedness in high places, according to Paul in Ephesians 6 v. 12. As I witnessed the transformation of my son, it saddened my heart even more. I began to feel the anguish of rejection, the loss of influence, the closeness that we had once shared as father and son. As time passed, he became more distant, more defiant in his rebellion. It was almost uncanny in what was taking place. Most of my time was now being devoted to upheavals in the family structure. The disruptions were beginning to affect the peace of the family as a whole. One by one, items from the home began to disappear with no apparent explanation. Without justification, I began to accuse my son, further widening the ever increasing gap that was already between us. I was not walking in the Spirit. I had condescended to the flesh, giving way to the very behavior that Paul warns fathers against in Ephesians 6 v. 4. He exhorts fathers not to provoke their children, but to bring them up in the nurture and admonition of the Lord. As a result of my provocation, he was pushed further into the clutches of the enemy.

"Because we wrestle not against the flesh, but against principalities and powers, spiritual wickedness in high places," I was reminded that spiritual warfare is *real*, and in the wake of this warfare, there are often casualties.

BATTLE LINES ARE DRAWN

As the circumstances mounted, there arose a sense of urgency within my spirit. The outward man still wanted to be in control of the situation, but the inward man was calling for a "release" unto God. Sometimes we hold onto things too tightly...even our burdens. There were burdens which I carried that I was not quite ready to give over to God. The "natural" part of me was still struggling with pride, while the spirit man within was saying, *"Let go!"*

It wasn't until late one summer evening that I experienced spiritual warfare on a level that I had not been accustomed. It came by way of a phone call, once again on my job. This time, my daughter was hysterical and audibly shaken. There was an eerie trembling in her voice, the likes of which I had never heard before. I couldn't quite make out what she was saying, so I asked her to put her mother on the phone. She did so, and my wife said, "Something's happening, and you need to come home right away!" My heart sank, and there was a sick feeling in the pit of my stomach, as if I was in mid "drop" on a roller coaster ride. I could hear the hysterical "shrieks" of my daughter in the background, as my wife attempted to calm her. I had no idea what was taking place at that moment, but according to my wife, our home seemed to be under siege! She shouted to me that it sounded as if someone were on the rooftop trying to gain entry to the house! I instructed her to hang up and call the police, as I dropped my phone and hurried home.

By the time I reached home, I found my wife and daughter huddled together in the kitchen; seemingly afraid to move. My daughter frantically tried to explain the situation, as my wife looked on in terror. The police had not yet arrived, and there was no visible sign of intruders other than huge stones lying in the yard. The sound that my wife had described to me earlier, were from the stones, as they were hurled at the house along the rooftop. I noticed that my son wasn't with them as we stood in the kitchen. When asked of his whereabouts, neither knew where he had gone. According to my wife, he wasn't there while all of the disruption was taking place. My immediate response was to pray. I gathered my wife and daughter together and held them close to me and began to pray a prayer of Divine protection over our family. Remembering the promises of God, and standing firm on His

Word was reassuring to both my wife and daughter. As the situation began to calm, I still had concerns about our son. Where was he? How long had he been gone? Was he alright? God only knew the answers. Later that night, he returned and told us that he had gone to visit a friend in the neighborhood. He was surprised to hear of what had happened earlier, and needless to say, we were both relieved that he was alright.

The following weeks brought even more chaos and mischief. During the course of this period, our home was further vandalized, along with both cars. By this time, these incidents were taking place both day and night; a relentless barrage of evil. The battle lines were drawn, and consequently, our family had become a target. I was reminded of a passage in Psalms 91 v. 5 which states, "Thou shalt not be afraid for the terror by night; nor for the arrow that flieth by day." Verse 6 elaborates in saying, "Nor for the pestilence that walketh in darkness; nor for the destruction that wasteth at noon-day." God's Word is timeless. It spoke to the situation we were currently facing. You see, during that time, the Word became more than just script on a page; but a very present help in time of trouble (Psalms 46:1). It became a type of salve in the soothing of our wounded spirits.

HEAR NO EVIL, SEE NO EVIL

Spiritual warfare is reflective of chaos in *heavenly* places. The heavenly places cannot be seen by the naked eye, but nevertheless; they exist. Ephesians 3 v. 10 speaks of principalities and powers which are located in heavenly places. In the book of Daniel, chaos erupted in heavenly places after Daniel petitioned God for an answer to his prayer. In Daniel 10 v. 12, the text proclaims from the "first day" that Daniel prayed and humbled himself before God, his words were heard, and God sent a messenger with his answer. However; in v. 13, the text explains that the messenger was held up for twenty-one days by the "prince of the kingdom of Persia." To put it simply, there was a struggle going on in the unseen that was soon to affect the outcome in the earthly realm.

There is a struggle going on in the "unseen" that affects us here in the earth. The "prince of the kingdom of Persia" in Daniel 10, is in reference to a demonic figure, assigned to influence that particular region in works of evil. The world we live in today is no different. There is demonic activity at work that influences our culture. It covers every area of life, be it social, political, economic, or religious. And yes, it particularly influences the family.

Family members are manipulated and separated because of demonic activity in the unseen realm of heavenly places. It is Satan's plan to attack and disrupt the family because it is representative of God's Divine order of family in heaven. The very word "chaos," according to Webster means "complete disorder, confusion, jumble — disarray." It is indeed Satan's intent to destroy the family, by fostering confusion, creating disorder...in order to *separate*.

THE SEPARATED SHEEP

Disobedience and rebellion cause separation from God. Just as Luke 15 spoke of the prodigal and his separation from his family, we sometimes separate ourselves from the flock. Whether it be rebellion, disobedience, or just plain curiosity, we find ourselves deep in the valley along those crooked paths where hidden dangers await. My son found himself along that pathway many times due to rebellion. It was only by the grace of God that he was sustained throughout his perilous journey. He chose to separate himself from the family and go his own way, unaware of the Destroyer which lie in wait for him.

It is the nature of any beast, when seeking to kill, to separate the weak from the herd or flock in order to satisfy his appetite. The enemy operates in much the same method as any other beast of prey. As a beast, preying on the weak, his chances of success are greater in a one-on-one confrontation. He is cunning, swift, and sure of his plan of attack. First he stalks his prey, being ever so careful as not to signal an alert, less his prey go on the defensive. His strategy is to use the element of surprise. Consequently, many of us fall prey to this strategy. The reason being is because the enemy's presence is so subtle. He is a master of disguise, and unless your spiritual eyesight is functioning at peak capacity, it can be difficult to see him coming. That's why Ephesians 6 v. 11 exhorts us to put on the whole armor of God that we might be able to stand against the wiles of the devil. He could come in the disguise of a friend, co-worker, neighbor, or family member. Because these are all familiar faces, we are more "relaxed" to some degree, which makes us vulnerable. Now granted, it is not the people themselves that we must be on guard against, but rather the source that influences them. Again, our struggle is not against flesh and blood, but against principalities and powers (Ephesians 6:12). Satan's strategy is to attack the mind in order to create doubt and confusion. This strategy proved to be effective in the Garden, and is still being used today. While creating this confusion, he manages to separate and divide families; leaving them vulnerable to attack.

It was Jesus Himself that said in Mark 4 v. 25, "And if a house be divided against itself, that house cannot stand." It is a statement that holds true in virtually any situation. There is a certain protection that comes with unity. Just as the church is strengthened by its members, so too is a family. When the members of each example are unified; they form a bond of security, inspiring one another, encouraging hope amongst its members. Without that security, hope is weakened, strength is diminished, and vulnerability is increased. In Luke 15, the prodigal mistakenly trusted in a false sense of security. He was secure as long as he had money to supply his needs. But eventually his money ran out. He put his trust in an idol, rather than the security that came from being in the presence of his father.

As my son was torn away from our family, he too came to realize the source of his hope, the foundation of his security, the support that is found through God's ordination of *family*. Enticed by the lures of peer pressure, and reinforced with a steady barrage of materialistic propaganda, it wasn't long before my son was convinced that the family was only keeping him from what he really wanted. It was a chance to have the freedom to choose his destiny. That is precisely what took place in Luke 15, as the father allowed his son the freedom to choose. Such was not the case in our situation however, as I struggled with feelings of guilt, pride, anger and humiliation as the course of events continued to unfold. The next several weeks would find the two of us seemingly isolated from reality, tossed about in a sea of confusion and uncertainty. There were days that were literally filled with chaos; each and every waking moment, a test of endurance. For several days at a time, my son would disappear, as if there were no consequence to his actions. He was now in full rebellion to the rule of authority. He had been introduced to life the way he thought it should be, and he wanted more of it.

As I struggled with emotions of despair and grief, I was reminded of II Corinthians 4 v. 8 as it states, "We are troubled on every side, yet not distressed; we are perplexed, but not in despair." Indeed I was perplexed at the sequence of events; they seemed to be relentless. There were many sleepless nights, brought on by anxiety, unaware of his whereabouts and concern for his safety. Inevitably, poor choices and disobedience led my son into a wilderness experience that neither of us would soon forget. Eventually, the seed of rebellion produced a consequential harvest. Galatians 6 v. 7

tells us, "Be not deceived; God is not mocked: whatsoever a man soweth, that shall he also reap." The seed had been sown, and now was the time for harvest. It came by way of several court appearances over the course of a year. As a father, I was appalled at having been placed in such a position of humiliation and degradation, as our family name was put to shame. But what was the real problem here? Was it my son's behavior or was God revealing a problem with my *pride*?

As I sat in on one particular courtroom appearance, I could not help but notice the long string of juveniles as they were "shuffled" into the courtroom. How sad it was to watch as they were all shackled together, with chains on both their hands and feet. As I watched, I could only think of the chains as being representative of Satan's grip on the youth of our society. Bound by oppression, rejection, and oftentimes depression, our youth struggle for identity. They follow the lures of the Evil One, and consequently pay a hefty price. They are the sheep that have been separated, cut off from the rest of the flock.....left as prey for the roaring lion.

Much to my horror, I sat and watched the mother of one of the juveniles stand up and vehemently shout of her disgust with her son, as his sentence was pronounced. She stormed out of the courtroom in a rage, vowing never to help or support him ever again. I thought to myself, "If Jesus had left us in the state of our sin, where would we all be?" How exceedingly glad we should be that we don't serve a God that gives up on us in our disobedience. How her son must have felt to hear those words, how he must have "cringed" at the thought of his mother abandoning him to be *ravaged* by the system, one of the separated....

As my son shook his head in disbelief, his head slowly turned to watch me, as if to say, "Will you react the same way? Are you going to walk out and leave me here all alone!" Staring straight into his eyes, with a slight smile on my face,

I gave a nod to reassure him that I wasn't going anywhere! It took a while for me to realize it, but God was trying to show me something throughout this whole ordeal. I had been taken out of the "box," out of that comfort zone that I had come to know so well. In retrospect, He was taking me down a path that had already been traveled, not just by other parents, but He was in some way, showing me what it was like for His Son; the shame, the ridicule, the humiliation that He endured on the Cross for our sake.

I mentioned earlier of the humiliation I felt because the family name had been compromised, the pain that I experienced through rejection, and the frustration I experienced behind my son's disobedience. Situations like these give us some insight as to the depth of God's grace and mercy which comes by way of His agape love. It is unconditional, without reservation. It isn't based on our behavior or performance. It is tied to the love that He has for His Son, because we have all been purchased by the blood of Jesus. He was a ransom for our sins (Matthew 20:28).

The sentence for my son was to spend three weeks in a juvenile detention facility. He didn't know this at the time, but this was God's way of getting his attention. It was through this God-ordained system of justice that allowed him to evaluate the path that he had chosen. Just like the prodigal in Luke 15, he suddenly took note of his surroundings and realized that he had lowered his standards. He was now living with the pigs, although not in a literal sense, but spiritually, he was lost.

THE REPENTANT PRODIGAL

Repentance is the first step toward restoration. The act of repentance is recognizing the wrong that has been committed and coming to grips with the inability to correct ourselves before a Holy God. To repent is to "turn away" from a particular behavior or pattern. Webster describes repentance as, "regret: to feel sorry for (something done)."

After three weeks of isolation and "desolation" in the "far country," my son came to repentance. During his stay, the only visitation that he received was from me. As I look back on that time, what an illustration it was, of God our Father, in relationship to us. I didn't realize it at the time, but what had already taken place in heaven, was now taking place on the earth! God said that He would never leave nor forsake us (Hebrews 13:5). Being placed as a steward over my son, the Lord used me to illustrate that promise to him.

As parents, we are representatives of God's love and mercy. In order to lead our children to God, we as parents must live according to God's Word. We are the visual representation of His Word *in action*. As we demonstrate His truth with consistency, our children will be more apt to follow. Even in those times when they find themselves in a far country, or perhaps in a dark valley; if we as parents have given them that "visual" picture of the Word in action, they will eventually be drawn back into the presence of the Father.

Sometimes it takes a traumatic event or chaotic circumstance to bring one to repentance. It is the nature of the circumstance that causes one to regret, to turn away from a particular behavior or mindset. The circumstances surrounding my son helped to bring him to repentance. It was a combination of that, coupled with the consistency of God's Word. You see, during my visits with him, I reminded him of God's plan for his life, regardless of the immediate circumstances. I was compelled as his father, to love him and to reassure him that he was not forgotten. In doing so, it is reflective of the nature of our Heavenly Father. He described his stay as one of misery. I recall a conversation that I had with him one evening over the phone. He said to me, "Dad, the rooms in this place are so hot, that I can't get any sleep." He even described the walls as "sweating" no doubt due to the humidity inside of the building. Whatever the reason, it was uncomfortable and he wasn't accustomed to that particular standard of living. As the prodigal in Luke 15, it caused him to reassess his situation.

Repentance can put us back on the correct path. As stated earlier, it is the first step toward restoration. When the prodigal in Luke 15 remembered the comforts of his father's house, he soon came to the conclusion that to be even a servant in his father's house would be better than where he was. My son came to learn that same lesson. We both learned something along the way. That opened the door to *restoration*.

RESTORING THE LOST

Restoration comes when genuine repentance takes place. Because the **Lord** is a God of mercy, He restores that which has been lost. **Joel 2 v. 25-26** speaks of His mercy in saying, "And I will **restore** to you the years that the locust hath eaten, the cankerworm, and the caterpillar, and the palmerworm, my great army which I sent among you. And ye shall eat in plenty, and be satisfied, and praise the name of the Lord your God, that hath dwelt wondrously with you: and my people shall never be ashamed."

The prodigal in Luke 15 was willing to return to his father after he had come to the end of *self*. He came to a point of helplessness and total depravity before he realized that he needed the security of his father. This is the point where most of us come to realize our dependence on God, the Father. When we come to the end of ourselves, when we've reached the end of our rope, we learn to submit ourselves before Him in repentance. In verse 18, the prodigal says, "I will arise and go to my father, and will say unto him, Father, I have sinned against heaven, and before thee." What did he do in making this statement? He *confessed* his sin. He came to the end of himself and he *repented* of his sin.

The Bible teaches us in I John 1 v. 9, "If we confess our sins, He is faithful and just to forgive us our sins, and to cleanse us from all unrighteousness." There has been some speculation as to the father's role in Luke 15. Some theologians would argue that the father acted foolishly in allowing the younger son to receive his inheritance prematurely. Still others argue that although it may have been premature, the father allowed his son the use of his own will in order to choose his own direction — perhaps in his wisdom, knowing that his son would return after exhausting himself in riotous living. Each scenario is subject to interpretation; but the underlying truth is that the son *did* return, and upon his return there was *forgiveness* on behalf of the father.

Throughout all of the difficulties, pain and hardships I've experienced with my own son, at the end of the day, there has always been forgiveness. It is a key factor in the restoration process. It is necessary if wounds are to heal and renewal is to take place.

REASONS FOR FORGIVENESS

There are many reasons why we should forgive. Although it is key in the restoration process of the person being forgiven, it is also linked to *our* being forgiven. Matthew 6 v. 14 says, "For if we forgive men their trespasses, your Heavenly Father will also forgive you." God is watching to see if we are forgiving one another. If we fail to forgive, then God will not forgive us of our transgressions (Matthew 6:15). Forgiveness is necessary, less we are delivered to our tormentors (Matthew 18:34). In this illustration given in Matthew 18, a servant was indebted to his lord. The servant was forgiven of his debt, but upon his release confronted another servant which was indebted to him. He failed to administer the forgiveness that had been extended to him. Because of his unforgiveness, the servant was thrown back in jail to answer to debt owed to his lord. Because he did not forgive, he was placed in bondage. When we fail to forgive, we too are placed in bondage. Forgiveness frees us to fulfill the purpose of God for our lives.

The father in Luke 15 showed forgiveness upon the return of his son. He expressed that forgiveness by instructing his servants to bring the best robe for his son to wear, a ring for his hand, and shoes for his feet. In doing so, he restored what the locusts had eaten (Joel 2:25), made the crooked paths straight (Luke 3:5), and released him of his guilt. How many parents are willing to do that for their children today? Regardless of what they may have done while away in a "far country," is it not prudent to forgive? The lack of forgiveness promotes chaos and limits growth. Luke 17 v. 3 says, "Take heed to yourselves: If thy brother trespass against thee, rebuke him; and if he repent, forgive him." If your child has repented of wrong doing, then forgive; that he or she may be released of the bondage of guilt and shame.

My son was no different than the prodigal in Luke 15. His exploits in the far country may have differed, but the end result was the same. After all was said and done, he returned home. Broken and repentant, he confessed the error of his ways. And because God had mercy on me when I was off into a far country, I extended that same mercy to my son.

CHAPTER FIVE

THE BENEFITS OF WISDOM

"Happy is the man that findeth wisdom, and the man that getteth understanding" (Proverbs 3:13)

When embroiled in the storms of chaos, one of our staunchest allies is that of *wisdom*. There are very few situations or circumstances where wisdom will not prove to be invaluable. God thought wisdom to be so important that the word itself is mentioned in Scripture over two-hundred thirty-three times. Perhaps the Lord placed so much emphasis on wisdom because to fear Him is the beginning of wisdom (Proverbs 9:10).

The bulk of the wisdom writings are contained in the books of Proverbs and Ecclesiastes. The book of Proverbs was authored by the wisest man that ever lived. That man was King Solomon, son of David, who was the greatest king Israel has ever known. Solomon was blessed in abundance with wisdom that came directly from God. According to Proverbs 2 v. 6, "The Lord giveth wisdom: out of His mouth cometh knowledge and understanding." Solomon received this wisdom, simply because he *asked* God for it. In the book of I Kings chapter 3, the Bible speaks of God coming to Solomon in a dream, bidding Solomon to ask of Him as he willed. Solomon, in the dream, having surveyed his inheritance through his father king David, realized the enormity of his inheritance. Feeling inadequate for the task ahead of him, faced with the rule over God's people, Solomon asks God for wisdom that he might have discernment to judge (I Kings 3:9).

Scripture states that God was so pleased with what Solomon had asked of Him that he not only granted Solomon wisdom and understanding, but he gave him riches and honor unlike any king of his day. His wisdom, the Bible says, was unlike anyone that had come before him, and there would be none after him that could compare (I Kings 3:12). We should all take a page from Solomon. In his request, he showed an immediate dependence on God for his success. Even though he had inherited a great deal, he acknowledged that God had shown David, his father, great mercy because he had walked in righteousness. You see, by observing how his father lived, Solomon "got it." He saw, through his father, that God was the source of his very existence. When we begin to live in relation to that revelation, it changes the way we think.

WISDOM VS. RICHES

A lack of provision can bring chaos, however; knowing that Christ has already made provision for the believer leads to one conclusion: there is a lack of knowledge. Because of that lack of knowledge Isaiah 5 v. 13 addresses the consequences saying, "Therefore my people are gone into captivity, because they have no knowledge: and their honorable men are famished, and their multitude dried up with thirst."

There are Christians today, who are in captivity to their finances because they lack knowledge and wisdom in accessing God's provision. Wisdom is the key to opening the door to that provision. Job 28 v. 18 proclaims that the price of wisdom is above rubies. Proverbs 16 v. 16 says, "How much better is it to get wisdom than gold! And to get understanding rather to be chosen than silver!" Why does Scripture emphasize wisdom over precious stones? Because it is God that gives the wisdom and knowledge to *find* the precious stones. Proverbs 4 v. 7 says, "Wisdom is the principal thing; therefore get wisdom: and with all thy getting get understanding." Verse 8 says, "Exalt her, and she shall promote thee: she shall bring thee to honor, when thou dost embrace her." In other words, when you have wisdom, coupled with understanding, it brings its own reward. For instance, if you were to take one hundred dollars, give it to a five year old child to invest, the likelihood of that investment being a good one is very low. On the other hand, if you were to take that same amount of money, and give it to a forty-something investment banker, the chances are greater for a good return. Why? Because the investment banker has experience that comes with age. The child hasn't had a chance to grow in respect to financial know-how.

Proverbs 12 v. 12 says, "With the ancient is wisdom; and in length of days understanding." Sadly though, financial provision in the hands of some Christians is comparable to the illustration of the five-year old. Because they lack the wisdom in the proper handling of the finances they often find themselves at a loss, stemming from poor decisions made concerning their finances. There are many people that receive family inheritances, that even by today's standards, would be considered as wealthy. But because of a lack of wisdom, within a few months, find themselves bankrupt, desperately trying to borrow money. There are numerous stories of lottery winners who suddenly become millionaires, only to become paupers within a couple of years. Why? First of all, lottery money for the Christian is ill-gotten money to begin with. The lottery is a game of *chance*, and to indulge in such a game is to deny God as being the source of their provision! For the Christian that has wisdom this truth is self-evident.

Furthermore, riches that are given of God require that we be good stewards. We must be faithful in that which is given for the advancement of His kingdom. However; those who come into financial prosperity who have no understanding may soon find themselves at a loss.

This is why it is so important to get wisdom, but in the process, to get *understanding*. The Bible says that wealth gotten by vanity shall be diminished: but he that gathers by labor shall increase (Proverbs 13:22). This verse speaks to many who have received wealth through vain avenues of life. The Hebrew root word for vanity is *habal*, which means "to be vain in act, word, or expectation — to lead astray." Many Christians are being led astray in the vain pursuit of false prosperity. They seem to have forgotten, that God supplies all of our needs according to His riches in glory by Christ Jesus (Philippians 4:19). He is Jehovah-jireh; translated from the Hebrew meaning, "the Lord provides."

In Genesis 22, Abraham was told to sacrifice his son, Isaac, to test his faith in God. He proved himself worthy, and in return God supplied a *substitute* for Isaac in the form of a ram. Abraham renamed Mt. Moriah and gave it the name of "Jehovah-jireh." With God as our provider why would we dare to live by chance? Proverbs 8 v. 18 proclaims, "Riches and honor are with me; yea, durable riches and righteousness." Wisdom tells us where to find *durable* riches: they are not fleeting, false, nor misleading. Durable riches are not gained by the scratch of a card, the pull of a slot handle, the spin of a wheel, or with the roll of the dice. For such is all vanity, and can be deceiving. Many have been led down the path to addictions caused by excessive gambling. The false hope of attaining "more" wealth in order to achieve "happiness" has fostered chaos.

The Bible clearly states, "Happy is he that hath the God of Jacob for his help, whose hope is in the Lord his God" (Psalms 146:5). As long as we have God as our help, there is no need to attach ourselves to false hope. He is the source of our provision, our Heavenly Father. It was with wisdom that God established the world (Jeremiah 51:15), and it is the Lord who gives wisdom, and out of his mouth comes knowledge and understanding (Proverbs 2:6). "He that trusteth in his riches shall fall, but the righteous shall flourish as a branch," proclaims Proverbs 11 v. 28. In today's society there are too many people that trust in their riches. They have bought into the deception of worldly justification. All too often, the world measures a person's net worth according to the size of their bank account. But God is not interested in how much money you will accumulate in this lifetime. His interest is in the heart; what you have done with what He has given. Will it be used for self-gratification or will it be used for His glory? Because some people are so preoccupied with achieving wealth the Word is often choked out of their lives.

Jesus gives an illustration in Luke 8 v. 14 when He says, "And that which fell among thorns are they, which when heard, go forth, and are choked with cares and riches and pleasures of this life, and bring no fruit to perfection." The verse is speaking of seed that is planted; that seed being the Word of God. As that seed falls amongst the thorns of life, it never really reaches the fertile soil, which is the heart. And because the cares of this world, along with its riches and pleasures interfere with the planting of that seed, it cannot be fully imbedded in the heart, thereby culminating in an unfruitful life. More time is spent in the pursuit of pleasure, than the pursuit of the kingdom. Matthew 6 v. 33 says, "But seek ye first the Kingdom of God, and his righteousness; and all these things shall be added unto you." God knows exactly what we need and when we need it.

WISDOM STRENGTHENS

When you are faced with a problem, a circumstance that you just can't seem to shake, you invariably seek a solution. You may go to a friend, a neighbor, a co-worker, or perhaps even a relative for advice. Everyone will give you their opinion; and perhaps all or none of the advice will suit your particular situation. But whatever the case may be, whether the advice is good or bad; what matters in the end, is what you do with it. You may choose to use it, but deep down inside you are still not sure that the advice received will remedy the problem. Eventually, you begin to experience periods of doubt, anxiety, and maybe even depression, as you begin to ponder the weight of your dilemma. In times like these, when you experience weakness, a chipping away of your inner strength; there is a friend that you can rely on: that friend is *wisdom*. Wisdom strengthens in the way of favor. Proverbs 14 v. 35 says, "The king's favor is toward a wise servant: but his wrath is against him that causeth shame." When you have wisdom, you have the favor of God. Daniel experienced that same favor. King Nebuchadnezzar, in Daniel chapter 2, had dreams that troubled his spirit, the Bible says. So the king summoned the magicians, the astrologers, sorcerers, and the Chaldeans, that they might interpret one particular dream. There was, however; one stipulation. The king required that not only were they to give the interpretation of that dream, but also had to reveal the actual dream itself. Realizing that what the king asked of them was an impossible request, the Chaldeans replied in verse 11 saying, "It is a rare thing that the king requireth, and there is none other that can shew it before the king, except the gods, whose dwelling is not with flesh." The Chaldeans were wise enough to know, that only the God of Glory could tell of the secrets of the soul. "Wisdom and might are His," declares Daniel 2 v. 10. The king, being furious with the response of his wise men, decreed that all of the wise men of Babylon would be destroyed. Daniel later convinced the king to give him time, and he would be able to reveal the king's mystery. After meeting with his companions, Daniel petitioned God for mercy, and to spare their lives. In response, God answered Daniel's request with the revelation of the king's dream. He received the favor of the Most High God.

Daniel received favor because he put his trust in God. There are too many people today that put their trust in the astrologers, tarot card readers, and fortune tellers. Just as in Daniel's time, they too are powerless to tell the secrets of the souls of men. What they offer is a "counterfeit" knowledge of something that has already been revealed to them by the person seeking their services. In Daniel 2 v.7, the magicians answered the king saying, "Let the king tell his servants the dream, and we will shew the interpretation of it." But the king resisted the request, feeling that if he were to tell of his dream, anything could be made up to tell of the interpretation. The king exhibited wisdom in his reasoning of the situation. If those of us today were to use the wisdom of God's Word, we would know to shun such practices to begin with. The Bible describes such practices as "witchcraft," and the children of God should have nothing to do with it.

Deuteronomy 18 vv. 10-12 state, "There shall not be found among you anyone that maketh his son or his daughter to pass through the fire, or that useth divination, or an observer of times, or an enchanter, or a witch, or a charmer, or a consulter with familiar spirits, or a wizard, or a necromancer. For all that do these things are an abomination unto the Lord: and because of these abominations the Lord thy God doth drive them out from before thee." God's Word is clear on the subject. Those who pretend to be able to tell your future are distorting truth. Only God is omniscient. Any revelation that is given to us in regard to our future are always tied to His Word. In relation to His Word, God has given the church, those gifted by the Holy Spirit, the gift of the *word of wisdom*. Being one of the nine gifts of the Spirit, it is often counterfeited by Satan in the form of *witchcraft*.

BEWARE OF COUNTERFEITS

In these days of deceit and trickery, we must constantly be on guard for counterfeits. They come in a variety of ways, but they always come with the intention of deception. So how do you guard against such deceit? First of all, equip yourself with the knowledge of the Word, so when the father of lies (who is Satan) comes knocking at your door, you will be prepared to answer with truth. Then allow the Holy Spirit to guide you as only He can. Without the wisdom and the knowledge of God it will be difficult to discern the counterfeit from the authentic. It is by way of the Holy Spirit, that you are led into all truth. As believers, it is imperative that we allow the Holy Spirit the freedom to function within our lives, as He can aid in the process of identifying these counterfeits. Well, you may say, "Just how is He going to do that?" The answer is simple. If we, knowing that this third Person of the Trinity, reveals the things of God (Isaiah 40:13, 14), and in fact, is our Helper (John 14:16, 26) and is indeed, the Spirit of God (Genesis 1:2), we can put our total trust in Him. The devil will always come with his deceit, but the Holy Spirit brings the power and anointing to overcome the deception. The power is in the Word, and the truth unveils the lie. I John 4 v. 4 says, "Ye are of God, little children, and have overcome them: because greater is He that is in you, than he that is in the world." As believers, the Spirit of God lives in us. He anoints us to discern the things of God (I Corinthians 2:10-16), and empowers us to make judgment (Micah 3:8). God does not want us to be ignorant. This is one of the reasons why He has given us the Holy Spirit — to teach and to guide us into truth.

In this world, we are literally surrounded by many spirits, both good (angels) and evil (demons). The angels represent God, along with His truth and righteousness. On the other hand, demonic forces represent Satan, and his diabolical schemes for the destruction of humanity, through deception. We are warned in I John 4 v. 1 of these deceptive spirits, and John tells us what we must do. He says, "Beloved, believe not every spirit, but try the spirits whether they are of God: because many false prophets are gone out into the world." Today, just as in John's time, there are many false prophets among us. So subtle are the ways of these "imitators" that they can be very difficult to detect. We are to detect them by "testing" them against the Word. I John 4 v. 2 says, "Hereby know ye the Spirit of God: Every spirit that confesseth that Jesus Christ is come in the flesh is of God."

THE SOOTHSAYER

The term "soothsayer," is defined by Webster as, "One who foretells events." Today, they are most commonly referred to as "fortune-tellers." Again, to reiterate, God's Word is perfectly clear on such practices. It is a counterfeit of the word of knowledge, which God gives by His Spirit. The fortune-teller's abilities are rooted in demonic sources. Paul had an encounter with a slave girl in Acts, chapter 16. Apparently, she had made lots of money for her masters by way of fortune-telling. Verse 16 reads, *"And It came to pass, as we went to prayer, a certain damsel possessed with a spirit of divination met us, which bought her masters much gain by soothsaying."* Scripture states, for several days she followed Paul and the men who were with him saying, "These men are the servants of the most high God, which shew unto us the way of salvation" (Acts 16:17). Finally, in verse 18, Scripture states that Paul, being grieved, turned to the *spirit* and commanded that it come out of the girl, in the name of Jesus Christ. "And it came out of her, that same hour." Notice that Paul spoke to the spirit that was in her. It was clearly *not* of God. The power that he used over the spirit was the name above all names, the Lord Jesus Christ. Jesus has authority over all powers, principalities, thrones and dominions (Colossians 1:16). Paul discerned that the spirit in the slave girl was not of God, and using the authority given to him by Christ, called it out!

How could Paul detect this particular spirit? Scripture doesn't tell us, but quite possibly he was led by the Holy Spirit. Paul, knowing the truth of God; reacted, based on his knowledge of God. The Scripture says that Paul was "grieved" as he turned to the spirit and commanded it to come out of the girl. The word "grieved" in the context of the Scripture is translated from the Greek, meaning "to worry" or "anguish — pain." Obviously Paul was upset due to the situation. But why? Was it because he knew what God's definitive Word stated? Perhaps, but there is another possibility. According to an explanation taken from *Nelson's Compact Bible Commentary*, editors Earl Radmacher, Ron Allen and H. Wayne House had this to say, "Paul was upset, not because what the girl said was untrue, but because the girl was being viewed as the source of truth." This statement seems to give a cogent explanation as to Paul's demeanor. This is precisely why God forbids the practice of fortune-telling. God is the *only* source of truth. Many Christians are deceived in thinking that consulting mediums is a harmless act, when in reality, it can be devastating. They are in the business of misleading people because they follow the lead of the one who is at enmity against God. He is recognized as the father of lies, his name – Satan. So don't be duped into thinking that just because one of these "soothsayers" professes to be a Christian that this is actually the case. "Satan himself is transformed into an angel of light," according to II Corinthians 11 v. 14. Remember, we must test the spirits by the Word (1 John 4:1). What has God said pertaining to the matter?

I once had an encounter with a fortune-teller in relation to my place of employment. In order to complete the task in which I had been assigned, it was necessary that I enter the premises. The premises from all outward appearances was clearly defined as a place of both *palm* readings and *tarot card* readings. Upon entry, I noticed a picture of Christ on the floor leaning against the wall. I was greeted by a rather petite woman that spoke with a very deep voice. I explained why I was there, but could not help but ask the question: "Do you believe in the Lord Jesus Christ?" Her reply to me was, "Yes, I am Christian." Knowing the truth of God, I replied, "Then tell me how you could operate in a business such as this, and still honor God?" She replied, "Because God gives some people the power to see the future."

Dr. Lester Sumrall in his book, *The Gifts and Ministries of the Holy Spirit*, had this to say regarding the power to see the future: "The word of knowledge is that gift given by God that allows a person to know something he cannot learn through his natural senses. God reveals it to his spirit. The devil, of course, would love to have people do that, too; only he uses false knowledge. The devil will "reveal" things, but his purpose is to trick you, to deceive you, to lead you into a trap."

Saints of God, be not deceived. Know the Word of God, and what it says. If God says to shun witches, warlocks, soothsayers, and all forms of divination, then be obedient to His Word. To fall prey to such deception only invites chaos into your life. As Christians, we know that God holds our future in His hands. We don't have to worry or fear what is to come, simply because He is in control. Our future doesn't depend upon horoscopes, tarot cards, or palm readings. It is solely dependent upon our obedience to His Word. We are led by His Spirit just as Paul was in Acts 16. He recognized the spirit of divination in the girl and commanded it to come out of her. Why? Because he knew the Word of God, and he was led by His Spirit, not that of a counterfeit!

WISDOM AND PROMOTION

There are many that work hard at what they do in order to receive a promotion from their employer. For some, it involves putting in long hours on the job, for others, it may require diligent study in order to become more knowledgeable so as to excel in a particular profession. But there is one particular attribute that aids in the promotion process; and that attribute is *wisdom*. "The wise shall inherit glory: but shame shall be the promotion of fools," according to Proverbs 3 v. 35. It is not uncommon to see that those who are diligent in their work, knowledgeable at what they do, but yet possess wisdom are often sought after for promotion. Perhaps it's because when a person of wisdom speaks, he speaks with a certain degree of knowledge. People tend to pay particular attention to the way words are spoken, as opposed to actual subject matter. On the other hand, a person that speaks foolishly is less likely to be taken seriously. The Bible says, "the tongue of the wise useth knowledge aright," meaning one who has wisdom knows what to say and when to say it.

Although wisdom is key when it comes to promotion, the Bible is expressly clear as to *where* promotion originates. Psalms 75 v. 6 says, "For promotion cometh neither from the east, nor from the west, nor from the south." Verse 7 expounds, "But God is the judge: He putteth down one, and setteth up another." This verse gives credence as to why the fear of the Lord *is* the beginning of wisdom. It's recognizing that all that we have comes from God. He is the source of wisdom. In Joshua 34 v. 9, Scripture states that he was *filled* with the spirit of wisdom. The verse goes on to read, "For

Moses had laid hands upon him: and the children of Israel harkened unto him, and did as the Lord commanded Moses." Joshua received promotion as he was filled with the spirit of wisdom." Scripture says the people "listened" to him and did as the Lord commanded Moses. An "impartation" of wisdom, a transference of power was released from Moses, a great man of wisdom, and deposited to Joshua by the "laying on" of hands.

How many times have we stopped to think about different situations in life when wisdom aided in promoting us. It may not have been in the context of a work-related promotion, but maybe there was a time or two when saying the right thing or doing the right thing, at just the right time, got you out of a tough spot. Wisdom played a role in that process. Wisdom made all the difference. For those who exalt wisdom, the Bible says, that they shall be promoted; and honor shall be brought to those who embrace her (Proverbs 4:8). Have you embraced wisdom today? Do so, and God will honor you.

WISDOM PRESERVES

Have you ever been in a situation where you were tempted to do something, but at the last minute changed your mind; just in time to avoid a disaster? If you have, then more than likely, you've experienced godly wisdom. Based on the knowledge that is placed in us by God, "the wisdom of the prudent is to understand His way: but the folly of fools is deceit," declares Proverbs 14 v. 8. When we understand what we are doing and why we are doing something, based on our knowledge of the situation, we are being guided by wisdom. On the contrary, the foolish are lost in their own deceit. They cast wisdom aside in lieu of vanity or wickedness. Take this illustration for example: A likely investor receives a phone call one day, concerning an investment deal; the chance of a lifetime. The caller informs him that the opportunity has been granted to him due to his exemplary credit rating and asks to set up an appointment to meet with him at a nearby office. The investor agrees to the meeting, and the next day, he arrives at the office. He notices that on his way there the location of the office is not in one of the most desirable sections of town; nevertheless, he is excited about the prospect of making this great investment.

Once inside the office, he notices that it is barely furnished and the paint is peeling off the walls. The prospective investor is greeted by a staff of three very friendly people who present to him a fairly well detailed plan that appears to have great promise. They show him a list of other would-be investors, some of which are from his own neighborhood. He is told that the window of opportunity is nearing a close, and he would have to act quickly in order to see his investment grow. At the last minute, he decides against the opportunity, citing that he needs more time to make a more informed decision. He leaves the office and decides to go home to pray on the matter to ask God for wisdom and guidance. Two days later, the prospective investor runs into one of his neighbors at a nearby grocery store, and they begin to discuss the investment opportunity presented by the investment firm across town. His neighbor tells him of a police sting operation that involved the same firm in question. It turns out that the staff members of the "so called" firm were arrested just one day after his decision to delay his response. Sound familiar? Although this was just an illustration, this type of scenario is played out all too often in real life. Because so many lack wisdom, they are susceptible to those with evil intent.

"Discretion shall preserve thee, understanding shall keep thee," proclaims Proverbs 2 v. 11. "Wisdom will keep you from the way of the evil man, from the man that speaks deception," as described in verse 12. Wisdom keeps us from falling into the snare. It preserves us that we may do the will of God. For those that turn away from it shall eat of the fruit of their own way and be filled with their own devices (Proverbs 1:31). Such was the case in the illustration. When wisdom is exalted, or exercised, it has the potential to deliver us from some of the snares of life. When properly applied, it can dispel deception. Proverbs 4 v. 6 says, "Forsake her not, and she shall preserve thee: love her and she shall keep thee."

HOW TO GET WISDOM

The first and obvious way to get wisdom is to fear the Lord. To fear God is to admonish who He is, to recognize His sovereignty, and to take His Word seriously. According to Psalms 111 v. 10, the fear of the Lord is the beginning of wisdom. James 1 v. 5 says, "If any of you lack wisdom, let him ask God, that giveth to all men liberally, and upbraideth not; and it shall be given to him." Notice that the verse says, that "it *shall* be given." It doesn't say that it might, or may *possibly* be given, but rather that it *shall* be given. We have to learn how to take God seriously at His Word. This is where wisdom begins. It is born of faith, fueled by trust in Him, and exalted through trial and perseverance. "For in much wisdom is much grief: and he that increaseth knowledge increaseth sorrow." So, if you are seeking to gain lots of wisdom, just be aware that the road will be paved with trials. In the process of sorrow and perseverance, *patience* will bear the fruit of wisdom.

Once you have attained wisdom, it is necessary to get understanding. This too, comes from God. Proverbs 1 v. 7 says that fools despise wisdom, but the fear of the Lord is the instruction of wisdom: and before honor is humility (Proverbs 15:33). If you are seeking true wisdom, then you must humble yourself before God. There are some in the world that exalt themselves in their own wisdom. But God says in I Corinthians 1 v. 19, "I will destroy the wisdom of the wise, and will bring to nothing the understanding of the prudent." There were scholars during the time of Christ that relied solely upon their intellect and reasoning skills to confront the problems of their day. They were known as the Pharisees. Just as they did in their time, so do some of today's scholars. But they do so in vain attempts to circumvent the wisdom and the knowledge of God. Some do so simply because they reject God, but yet others do so out of vanity. It is the feeble attempt of man to gain the favor of God through intellect, rather than coming to the realization that man has fallen short of the glory of God and can only be justified by faith alone, which was made possible by the sacrifice of the Lord Jesus Christ upon the Cross.

Paul makes it clear in Romans chapter 3, that justification is by faith. Martin Luther confronted a similar problem in his day, which gave birth to the reformation of the early church. The way to get wisdom is by first *fearing* God, *submitting* to His will, *humble* yourself before Him, *ask* Him for wisdom, and *receive* it by faith.

WISDOM DIRECTS

"If the iron be blundt, and he do not whet the edge, then must he put to more strength: But wisdom is profitable to direct." (Ecclesiastes 10:10)

There is no secret that we live in what is referred to as a post-modern era. Christianity is under attack like never before in every facet of the culture. The very mention of God in some places is enough to offend someone, and in some cases, invite frivolous lawsuits designed to silence the Christian community. But God did not give us a spirit of fear, but rather a Spirit of power and of love and a sound mind (II Timothy 1:7). Because we, as believers, have the Spirit of

God within us, we have a Spirit of wisdom. I Corinthians 1 v. 30 speaks to this in saying, "But of Him are ye in Christ Jesus, who of God is made unto us wisdom, and righteousness, and sanctification, and redemption." The same Spirit that works within us is the same Spirit that guides us into all truth (John 16:13). As believers, we have the wisdom of God through Christ, to help us to navigate through the rough areas of life. Unfortunately, many Christians are not aware of the work of the Holy Spirit.

Genesis 1:2 describes the Holy Spirit as the "Spirit of God." In John 14:17 He is recognized as Truth. John 14:16, 26 describe Him as the Helper. He is called God in Acts 5:3-4, recognized as Eternal, in Hebrews 9:14, is joined with the Father and Son in Matthew 28:19, speaks in Acts 28:25, teaches in John 14:26, comforts in Acts 9:31, gives gifts in I Corinthians 12:3-11, illuminates the mind (I Corinthians 2:12-13), reveals the things of God (Isaiah 40:13-14), and many more attributes that are numerous in scope.

Today, it is more important than ever that we heed the guidance of the Holy Spirit because the days are evil. The persecution of the church has escalated at a phenomenal rate. Absolute truth is being rejected by the culture at large; evil is being looked upon as good, and good for evil. The Bible has plenty to say regarding these things, but the most chilling statement comes out of Isaiah 5 vv. 20 and 25. "Woe unto them that call evil good, and good evil; that put darkness for light, and light for darkness; that put bitter for sweet and sweet for bitter," states verse 20. Then verse 25 paints a graphic picture of the anger of the Lord saying, "Therefore is the anger of the Lord kindled against His people, and He hath stretched forth His hand against them and hath smitten them: and the hills did tremble, and the carcasses were torn in the midst of the streets. For all this, His anger is not turned away, but His hand is stretched out still." What graphic detail, what a sobering description of the horror that awaits those who would willfully and woefully commit such atrocities against the Almighty God. Let there be no mistake in the interpretation of God's intent in that verse. His wrath will be poured out on a perverse nation that rejects His Word of truth.

WISDOM TO DISCERN

One of the gifts of the Holy Spirit is the gift of the discerning of spirits. There is a sinister spirit of antichrist at work in the earth today. Its purpose — to distort the truth of God and spread deception amongst the members of the body of Christ in order to create confusion. While speaking with a friend recently, he brought to my attention the fact that such a spirit is indeed prevalent within the church. Now, this in itself is no surprise, knowing that spiritual warfare revolves around the very truth of God. The thing that was so alarming was the enormity of the amount of damage inflicted by this spirit, and its capacity for deception. My friend, being relatively new as a believer, is hungry for the truth of God. He is diligently seeking the kingdom and wants to worship the Lord in spirit and in truth. With this being the case, just as it states in Mark 15 v. 5, "Satan comes to steal the Word that is sown into their hearts." The verse reads, "And these are they by the way side, where the Word is sown; but when they have heard, Satan cometh immediately, and taketh away the Word that was sown in their hearts." Jesus was speaking of seed that was being sown. The seed in the illustration is the Word of God. Satan will always try to steal or diminish the Word so it cannot be used to empower the believer.

INSTRUMENT OF DECEIT

Some time ago, my good friend and brother in Christ, presented to me an article that he retrieved from the internet regarding what appeared to be a "self-proclaimed" prophet of

God. In the article, this "prophet" named several evangelical leaders and numerous churches, both past and present, that are supposedly responsible for the "division" amongst the body of Christ. He claims to have heard from Christ "specifically" concerning a particular matter involving the church, and that he had been chosen to relay this message, as it pertains to the body. According to I Corinthians 14 v. 29, prophets are to speak by two or three and the other is to judge. Verses 32 and 33 state, "And the spirits of the prophets are subject to the prophets. For God is not the author of confusion, but of peace, as in all churches of the saints." That pretty much says it all. God is *not* the author of confusion. We must not forget to "test" the spirits to see if they are of God. To my knowledge, the author of the article mentioned earlier is a "lone voice in the wilderness."

Whether some would agree or disagree with this man's conclusions, one thing was certainly evident: the greatest division amongst the body of Christ is fueled by such articles as was presented to me. This self-proclaimed prophet and supposed "scholar" (level of degree behind his name) managed to take the two Scriptures that he used in defense of his "research" entirely out of context in order to serve *his* particular purpose. If that wasn't enough, to go one step further, he printed the words that Jesus "supposedly" spoke to him, in *red* lettering, as if these words were Scriptural. This is one of the reasons why we *must* study Scripture for ourselves that we might be able to expose the counterfeits when they arise.

The question is, how do you distinguish what is truth and what is not? Scripture says, "Sanctify them through thy truth: thy word is truth" (John 17:17). John 16 v. 13 says the Spirit of God will guide you into all truth. John 8 v. 32 states, "And ye shall know the truth, and the truth shall set you free." These are all quotations from God's Word. His *Word* is the gauge by which we are to test the spirits. Because we live in a world literally filled with spirits, both good and evil, we are told to "believe not every spirit, but try the spirits whether they are of God: because many false prophets have gone out into the world" (I John 4:1). The intention of the writer of the article, as interpreted, was to expose false prophets, but in reality he planted seeds of doubt into my friend's mind causing him to question the validity of the Gospel. Ask yourself this question: Was this a *good* thing? The author quite literally exposed *himself* in the misuse of God's Word. You see, it was the Word that exposed his scheme. Matthew 7 v. 20 says, "Wherefore by their fruits ye shall know them." The fruit that was brought to bear was "bitter." It wasn't an article of unity, but rather one of "division." The article caused *confusion*. God's Word brings clarity. The so-called "prophet" spoke alone. And now, he is subject to the other prophets.

LESSONS TO REMEMBER

The incendiary nature of the article stirred up a righteous anger within me; one that prompted a quick lesson in apologetics. I mounted an effort to undo the damage that was caused by the article, supplying my friend with biblical truth, as opposed to misguided conjecture. Again, the real issue is not whether the subject matter of the article was true or false, but rather, how do we as believers determine what to take in and what to discard? We have to immerse ourselves in Scripture so that our spirits are saturated with His truth. As believers in Christ, we have been born of an incorruptible seed (I Peter 1:23), that seed being the seed of God. Because God works in us both to will and to do of his good pleasure, according to Philippians 2 v. 13, we have been endowed with a Spirit of wisdom and revelation in the knowledge of Him (Ephesians 1:17). If we are to be effective for the kingdom, we must use every tool that has been given to us by God, in order to dispel the kingdom of darkness.

When Jesus was tempted by Satan, in Matthew 4, He did not flee, nor did he question the Tempter. He resisted him by simply stating what God *said*, as opposed to what He was being led to believe. His statements began with the words "It is written" because Jesus knew the Word. Not only did He know the Word, He was the Word made flesh (John 1:14). The knowledge and wisdom of God the Father was working within Him to guide and instruct because the fullness of the Godhead dwelled within Him (Colossians 2:9). With the Holy Spirit working in us the only thing that we should be led to believe is the truth of God! When we study to show ourselves approved in order to rightly divide the Word (II Timothy 2:15), we will not be so easily deceived by everything we hear or see.

Paul, in his letter to the Ephesians addressed this very problem. He wrote in chapter 4 v. 14, "That we henceforth be no more children, tossed to and fro, and carried about with every wind of doctrine, by the sleight of men, and cunning craftiness, whereby they lie in wait to deceive." When we know what the Word of God says, and are led by His Spirit, wisdom will alert us to error when it rears its ugly head. Red flags should go up in the hearts and minds of those who are called according to His purpose. We are to examine the evidence and test it by His Word. If it does not line up with His Word, then it should be dismissed! If for whatever reason, difficulties arise concerning the interpretation of Scripture, we have the Holy Spirit working in us to give illumination to God's Word (I Corinthians 2:12, 13). We have only to ask of God for the wisdom needed (James 1:5) so that we can apply His Word to serve His purpose.

THE FINAL ANALYSIS

In light of the situation concerning my friend, it is important to state that situations such as these are indicative of the times in which we live. Although currently, our nation is involved in a war which can be perceived by the naked eye, it is reflective of another war — one that is undetectable by human abilities. It is a spiritual war, and can only be discerned by way of the Spirit. We live in an information age where there seems to be no limit to the amount of information we can obtain. But in our quest for information, we must consider that not *all* information is necessarily good information. The truly good information that we can rely on is the Word of God. It alone is inerrant and infallible, and *proven* to be true. When we receive information, we must always consider the source from which it comes. The article that was mentioned earlier was authored by a gentleman who happened to be a guest on a local radio program. The show has a segment in it where its prime goal is to expose error within the church. As callers call in to this show, they discredit the church by pointing out flaws in the church leadership. The host of the show even seems jovial in his attempts to get more callers to respond. Several questions cry out for answers, namely these: What does this do to build up the body of Christ? Does not the church itself *still* belong to Christ? Are we, as believers not *all* members of the body? And finally, is Christ not still the head of that body? Perhaps these are questions that the author, as well as the host, should have examined before airing such atrocities against the church. Psalms 75 v. 7 states, "But God is the judge: He putteth down one, and setteth up another." God Himself gives people their places of authority, and if they abuse it, then *He* will see that they are removed!

As situations such as these arise, it is all the more reason why we should know the Word for ourselves. While there is such a gift of prophecy (I Corinthians 13:2), God still speaks to us through His Son. The work that was done on the Cross, and all that He accomplished is in the Word. The purposes of the spiritual gifts, which come by way of the Holy Spirit, are for the *edification* of the church and the *building up* of the saints. The article that was written, and the radio program, both did very little for the building up of the saints. By using God's Word to "test" the spirits (using what God says in His Word, as opposed to what we're led to believe), the fruit of the *Accuser* is brought to bear in this example.

As a result of such spectacles of "gossip" callers respond by making such comments as, "That's exactly why I don't attend church" or "That's the reason why I don't trust these pastors." What purpose does it serve to neglect the church body? Are we not called to assemble with one another for the purpose of exhortation and encouragement (Hebrews 10:25)? Doesn't the Word tell us that faith comes by hearing the Word of God (Romans 10:17)? If this is true, then the question remains, "How can we hear the Word, without the benefit of listening to a preacher?" Again, examine the fruit that was produced by the skepticism of the critics. Does it fall in line with God's Word? In this case, apparently not. Its harvest was that of bitter fruit, and its only profit goes to serve the kingdom of darkness. Those who do not know the truth are void of understanding. They lack wisdom, and as a result, are blinded by the god of this age, who is Satan. II Corinthians 4 v.4 speaks explicitly to this in saying, "In whom the god of this world hath blinded the minds of them which believe not, lest the light of the glorious Gospel of Christ, who is in the image of God, should shine unto them."

So you see, the enemy has many devices at his disposal to use against the church. Scripture states that he comes disguised even as an "angel of light," which tells us that he is able to transform himself for the purpose of deception. II Corinthians 11 v. 15 has this to say regarding the false prophets: "Therefore it is no great thing if his ministers also be transformed as the ministers of righteousness; whose end shall be according to their works." The "works" of an individual will eventually give way to his or her ultimate motivation or intent. The Word, being the gauge by which we base our judgment, will expose the intent of the wicked. And for those who are not sure if they are being used by the enemy, maybe it's time to re-establish that relationship with Christ. For He is *filled* with knowledge and wisdom!

CHAPTER SIX

THE STEWARDSHIP OF TIME

"To everything there is a season, and a time to every purpose under the heaven." (Ecclesiastes 3:1)

We live in a very hectic world today, one that places demands on our *time*. So much so, that the element of time is often taken for granted. As an integral part of God's plan for human existence, it has often been misused, and at times, taken for granted. Time was created by God for mankind as God Himself is an infinite Being. He is self-existent, Eternal God, I AM THAT I AM, the One who has no beginning and no end, yet He is the Alpha and the Omega, the beginning and the end (Revelation 21:6). Simply stated, God always was, still is, and always will be! He is outside of time. He does not merely exist, nor does He *live* outside of time: He simply is....

Because God has created the element of time He undoubtedly created it for a purpose. That purpose is so that you and I would accomplish His will in the context of our allotted time. Notice that the statement reads "allotted time." That suggests that there is a *limit* placed on our time. It is not indefinite, nor unlimited, but it is without a doubt, *appointed*.

Yes, time is appointed, at least as far as it pertains to our time here on earth. Hebrews 9 v. 27 gives testimony to the fact that our time on earth is limited. It states, "And as it is appointed unto men once to die, but after this, the judgment." This statement has very clear implication that there is no such thing as "reincarnation," returning to this life in the form of some animal or another human being. The "judgment" refers to the judgment of Christ, as He will judge both the wicked and the righteous at the appointed time (I Peter 4:5).

We generally don't like to think of death. It is often linked with finality, conclusion — non-existence. But for the believer, death is merely a door to eternity, and to step through that door is to step into the presence of Almighty God for all eternity.

A TIME FOR EVERY PURPOSE

Did you know that we have been created for a purpose? Many people spend their whole lives searching for that purpose. Most often, the searching is in vain primarily because they have overlooked the One who gives us purpose — the Lord Jesus Christ. He reveals to us the mystery of the will of God. This, He has purposed in Himself, according to Ephesians 1 v. 9. Paul further speaks of this mystery in Ephesians 3 v. 9 as something that is *hidden* in God who created all things by Jesus Christ. For those who may be tempted or even intrigued to know the mystery behind the "secret" of life's purpose, just remember that it can only be found in Jesus Christ. He is the key that unlocks the mystery. Any other means is a counterfeit.

Man, in and of himself, is incapable of knowing the mysteries of God. In Christ lies the eternal purpose for mankind. So, in order to find out what our purpose is in this lifetime, we must first come to Jesus, as the eternal purpose is wrapped up in Him alone. Knowing that the mystery of the will of God is waiting for us in Him, why would we even want to search elsewhere? So the question remains, when is the time to discover this purpose? The time is now. No time is too soon to discover your purpose in Christ. Our purpose is to serve Him both here in the earth and throughout eternity. It was Christ who paid a ransom to the Father for the sins that we committed. He was crucified, dead, and buried; but He rose from the dead, having broken the power of sin and having paid the penalty for sin. He did this so that we could have life and have it more abundantly. God, the Father, purposed this very thing through His Son. Yes, — now is the time to discover your purpose!

AN EVIL TIME

It takes very little discernment, given a glimpse of today's media headlines, to know that we are living in an evil time. There are wars and rumors of wars. There is also famine, pestilence, wickedness and abominations of every kind in our world today. Chaos seems to have penetrated every facet of society just as in the days of Noah. Unfortunately, just as those days brought judgment upon the earth, our present time will undoubtedly face God's judgment. We've learned from this great lesson in Genesis that none were saved from destruction except for the righteous: the righteous at that time being Noah and the members of his family.

When times are evil, chaos abounds. Panic and fear sweeps across the human mind, giving birth to reasoning and imaginations. The Bible tells us to cast these things down because they exalt themselves against the knowledge of God (II Corinthians 10:5). We are to bring every thought into captivity and to the obedience of Christ. Why are we to do this? Because the battle is in the mind. Remember Adam and Eve in the Garden, and the enemy's first plan of attack?

It was to take control of the mind — the very thoughts that were placed in their minds became corrupt. Why? Because the *enemy* placed them there. This is why, as believers, we must take every thought captive and bring them to the obedience of Christ. So often, we fear what we cannot understand, but God has given us wisdom, and He imparts His knowledge to us through His Word. We have a tendency to react to the circumstance without the knowledge of His Word. This only breeds more confusion.

A TIME OF AFFLICTION

To every person there comes a time of affliction; a time of distress, anguish — tribulation. When such a time arises; that person may feel lost and afraid. He may exhibit a sense of helplessness. Sometimes the effects of an affliction can isolate or separate us from friends and loved ones. It can cause us to retreat into the inner sanctity of bewilderment searching for answers that can only be found in Christ. Jesus was described as a "Man of sorrows," in Isaiah 53 v. 3, because He was despised and rejected of men: He was acquainted with grief, according to the text. Certainly, Jesus was afflicted with the enormous burden of taking the sins of the world upon Himself. In fact, the affliction was so great that just prior to His arrest He asked God, the Father, for another way to accomplish His purpose. Matthew 26 v. 42 reads: "He went away again the second time, and prayed, saying, O my Father, if this cup may not pass away from me, except I drink it, thy will be done." Although Jesus suffered His affliction, He relinquished His will to that of the Father. It is important that in our time of affliction, that we too learn to relinquish our will to God, the Father.

When we are afflicted, whether it be through trials, persecution or circumstances, we search for another way, another path that we may take in the hope of somehow avoiding or perhaps escaping the inevitable consequences that lie before us. The time of affliction can be painful, stressful — even agonizing to the point of despair. Paul knew despair, as he addressed the church in Corinth. In II Corinthians 1 v. 8, he spoke of disparity of life itself. His words stated, "For we would not, brethren, have you ignorant of our trouble which came to us in Asia, that we were pressed out of measure, above strength, insomuch that we despaired even of life." How many of us have come to that crossroad, that dreadful place in the annals of despair that beckons for surrender, to give up the fight —to succumb to life's pressures. Have you ever been pressed out of measure above your own strength? Many of us have experienced such an ordeal in the form of pressures on the job or perhaps a wayward child, a debilitating sickness or disease. Perhaps you are the primary caregiver of an aging adult parent or loved one. These examples can often test the limits of human endurance. These are the times when it can seem that we are "pressed out of measure."

Sometimes the weight of our afflictions can be so intense that at times it can seem almost unbearable. But Jesus gives us the perfect example as to what to do when such a time comes. He submitted Himself to the will of the Father for He knew that the Father's way was perfect. According to II Samuel 22 v. 31, "As for God, His way is perfect; the Word of the Lord is tried: He is a buckler to all them that trust in Him." The question is do we trust in God enough to submit to His will? Sometimes His will requires us to face agony and endure pain — to suffer hardships that we might be *refined*. Sometimes it is necessary that we be "pressed out of measure" so that we may be molded into the image of Christ. Just as tempered steel requires intense heat in the refining process, the heat of our afflictions help to shape us.

THE FURNACE OF AFFLICTION

Although affliction can be painful, it is often necessary to "burn away" excess "baggage." When the intensity of our afflictions seems too much for us to bear, God is willing to step into that furnace and strengthen us to the point where we are able to "stand" in His strength as He sees us through the refining process. Shadrach, Meshach, and Abednego experienced the refiner's furnace when king Nebuchadnezzar had them tossed into it for failure to worship him. The Bible says the flames were so hot that as the doors of the furnace were opened the guards were incinerated (Daniel 3:22). Scripture also states that the king returned the next morning expecting to find only the ashes of the three young men that he had ordered to be thrown into the fiery furnace. Instead, much to his amazement, he saw four figures "walking" in the midst of the fire (Daniel 3:25). Isn't that just like God to be faithful and true to His Word? Even in the pain of our affliction in the depths of our valleys and in the fiery furnace of tribulation, He said that He would never leave nor forsake us (Deuteronomy 31:8). The king spoke to them from the mouth of the furnace and told them to come out, but only three of them exited. Needless to say that the king was astonished to not only see that the men were still alive, but they had not suffered any damages from the intense heat of the furnace. When the heat gets turned up in our fiery trials, if we are in Christ, they are designed to strengthen us.

According to Daniel 3 v. 27, "The fire had no power, nor was an hair on their head singed." The verse also says that, "not even the smell of fire had passed on them." How was this possible? First, they believed by faith that God was in control of their circumstance, then they committed to His Divine lordship, and finally submitted to His will. When we find ourselves facing overwhelming adversity, we must remember that God is *always* in control. "The name of the

Lord is a strong tower: the righteous runneth into it, and is safe," proclaims Proverbs 18 v. 10. When we encounter adversity, we must learn to call on the name of the Lord. Because He is a strong tower in our time of trouble, we can be safe, knowing that we are grounded in the foundation of His Word.

In the case of Shadrach, Meschach, and Abednego, God saw their commitment to Him even in the face of their affliction. Isaiah 48 v. 10 exemplifies their actions on stating, "Behold, I have refined thee, but not with silver; I have chosen thee in the furnace of affliction." Did you know that God chooses us in the furnace of affliction? In the midst of our pain and suffering, He chooses to do His greatest work in us. You see, it is in the furnace of affliction where our weaknesses are exposed, laid bare before Almighty God. Excess "baggage" is lifted and the heart is revealed.

Throughout Scripture, fire is described as a consuming element. It is often linked with purification. It is I Corinthians 3 v. 13 that proclaims, "Every man's work shall be made manifest: for the day shall declare it, because it shall be revealed by fire; and the fire shall try every man's work of what sort it is." Simply stated, our true work will be put to the test. A fiery trial will reveal whether or not we "walk the walk" or simply "talk the talk." Remember, the fire burns away the excess so that the heart is laid bare. From that point God begins the molding process. Malachi 3 v. 3 states, "And He shall sit as a refiner and purifier of silver: and He shall purify the sons of Levi, and purge them as gold and silver, that they may offer unto the Lord an offering in righteousness." Have you been purged by the refiner's fire? Has the heat of your affliction driven you before the altar of the Almighty God? If so, then you are acquainted with the purging process. As the heat of the affliction is turned up, the chaff is consumed. It is burned by an unquenchable fire (Matthew 3:12), one that melts the very core of your being. When our faith has been tested, tried by the fire of affliction, then we shall be able to give glory and honor to the Lord Jesus Christ (I Peter 1:7).

A TIME OF WAR

The prospect of war is not a very popular subject, and understandably so, as its result usually brings about some form of destruction. The very premise of war is generally conceived from conflicting ideals of the parties involved, which culminate in eventual confrontation. As distasteful as the prospect of war is; sometimes it becomes necessary to engage in it. The entrance of sin into the world gave way for the existence of evil. Unfortunately, evil is persistent, and will not be diminished until it is effectively dealt with. With that being the case, war is frequently, although not always, the end result. As mentioned earlier in chapter 2, "The Birth of Chaos," the earliest recorded warfare began in heaven itself as a result of two conflicting ideals — one being the absolute rule and supremacy of Almighty God, while the other was consistent with the envious and prideful rebellion of the lesser created angelic beings. Exodus 15 v. 3 depicts God Himself as a "Man of war." It states, "The Lord is a Man of war. The Lord is His name." While it is clear that the Lord is not a man, but indeed Spirit, the author conveys to us in this statement that Jehovah God is a God of justice.

Moses exalted God in his praise for the manner in which He defended the children of Israel against Pharoah at the Red Sea. God revealed Himself as Jehovah God. Nathan Stone, the author of the book, "Names of God" speaks of the righteousness of God through one of His many names. He is quoted as saying, "Jehovah created man to enjoy and to exhibit His righteousness. So, He demands righteousness and justice and holiness from the creatures made in His image. It is as Jehovah that He looks upon a wicked and corrupt earth and says, "I will destroy." Pharoah and his army were drowned in the Red Sea. All resulted from an act of Jehovah God — the righteous and true God of justice. God Himself went to war for His people because He is just.

What a powerful metaphor this Old Testament story represents. With their backs up against the sea, surrounded on either side by mountains, and Pharoah's army drawing ever closer, they had absolutely no place to go. But God was with them and He made the battle His own. He revealed Himself in the glorious splendor of His righteousness and justice for His name's sake. Not only did He prove to the children of Israel that He could be trusted, but He proved to His enemies that His wrath is to be feared! Because God is the same God today as He was at the Red Sea He awaits to prove Himself to a stubborn generation that have yet to believe that He is the King of Glory. When we find ourselves surrounded by a barrage of life's difficulties that at times seem to threaten our very existence, we can rely on God to see us through. Pride oftentimes pits us against the enemy without the assistance of God. This often ends in disaster. Have you ever attempted to tackle a serious problem in life without the benefit of the counsel of God? Perhaps you have and maybe even had some measure of success. Or maybe you've experienced a significant degree of failure. Whatever the case, putting your trust in God insures complete and total victory.

Moses was instructed to tell God's people in Deuteronomy 1 v. 42 not to confront the enemy without Him, but they disregarded His instruction. Moses' words were, "And the Lord said unto me, say unto them go not up, neither fight; for I am not among you; lest ye be smitten before your enemies." As you confront your daily challenges, are you petitioning God for His counsel? Are you awaiting His instruction for the next strategy in your battle? Psalms 24 v. 8 asks the question, "Who is the king of glory? The Lord strong and mighty, the Lord mighty in battle."If you happen to be the type that likes to "go at it" alone, just remember that if you choose to do so, you risk the possibility of disastrous results. Allow the Lord to fight your battles. His strength is a perfect strength indeed for who can challenge the Lord God Almighty?

A TIME TO MOURN

To mourn is to lament; to grieve for; to wear the customary habit of sorrow, according to Webster. The death of a loved one is certainly the most recognized occasion to mourn. When Jacob was led to believe that his son Joseph had been torn to shreds by an evil beast, as described in Genesis 37 vv. 33 and 34, he *mourned* the loss of his son. Although Joseph did not actually come to such demise, his father reacted based on what he was led to believe. He mourned, due to the absence of his son; someone that he loved and was very close to had been taken away from him.

Mourning does not necessarily equate to a physical death. We sometimes find ourselves mourning a *spiritual* death as well. For instance, some parents sometimes find themselves in anguish concerning a prodigal child. They "grieve" the path the child has chosen, and therefore they mourn for his or her soul. Another example is one of a corporate nature: A once powerful and influential company executive loses his or her position, resulting in a loss of authority. The former executive may mourn the loss of that authority as it carries with it a certain degree of power. To have such power for a given time, and then to suddenly lose that power, sometimes gives reason to mourn. Both examples are commonly joined together by "grief." When we find ourselves grieving, usually "death" in some form is within arm's reach. Someone or something has died, and mourning death brings separation, whether it be physical or spiritual, and the loss of someone or something that will be missed. Whatever the case may be, the fact remains that there is an appropriate time to mourn.

A TIME TO DIE

Death is a subject that many of us would rather not ponder. However, as grim as the thought of it may be, consequently, it is a reality of life. The reality of death is depressing to most of us because death itself causes "separation," and separation often magnifies a sense of loss. The loss of a loved one can cause feelings of anxiety and depression, periods of bitterness, remorse, sorrow and fear — fear of the unknown, as we struggle to understand the sovereignty of God in such a definitive issue. God Himself has determined our time here on earth (Psalms 37:18), and that determination falls within His Divine providence. But even as death unleashes residual effects, such as pain, fear, grief, sadness, and sorrow, the reality of God's Word has promised the believer eternal life. As one of the most cherished promises of God, we embrace the thought of someday reuniting with loved ones that have gone on before us. It is the hope that we have in Christ Jesus, as He is the firstborn from the dead (Colossians 1:18), meaning that He is the first to be resurrected from the dead. His resurrection is what gives us (the church body) hope that we too shall be raised at the appointed time.

Interestingly enough, Scripture records at least nine resurrections, three of which were performed by Jesus. Among the most notable is the raising of Lazarus (John 11:43). When Jesus heard of Lazarus' death, he made a profound statement in John11 v. 4 saying, "This sickness is not unto death, but for the glory of God, that the Son of God might be glorified thereby." God had a purpose, even in the death of Lazarus. Jesus waited for two additional days after receiving news of Lazarus, and by the time He arrived at his gravesite, Lazarus had already been dead for four days. Jesus' intent in His delayed response was to exhibit the miraculous resurrecting power of the Godhead. He replied in John 11 v. 42, "And I knew that thou hearest me always: but because of the people which stand by I said it, that they may believe that thou hast sent me." Jesus openly demonstrated the resurrecting power of God for the expressed benefit of convincing the people that He was sent by the Father.

A TIME TO HEAL

In resurrecting Lazarus, Jesus did two very important things. One thing He did was to call Lazarus by name. His command in John v. 43 was "Lazarus, come forth." Had He not called him by name the awesome resurrecting power of God may very well have awakened the entire cemetery! The second thing He did was to show that the power of God has the ability to restore life to what is believed to be dead. Is there something in your life that has been given up for dead? Are there hopes, dreams and visions that the enemy has managed to destroy or perhaps kill off? Maybe there is a loved one that you may have written off long ago because of a drug or alcohol addiction.

Whatever the case may be, Jesus is able to restore those hopes and dreams, to breathe life back into dead relationships, to resurrect that which was buried. He proved to us what He can do if we believe. Jesus said to Martha, the sister of Lazarus in v. 40, "Said I not unto thee, that, if thou wouldest believe, thou shouldest see the glory of God?" If we would only believe, we could see the glory of God made manifest in restored relationships, renewed hope, and the resurrection of dreams and visions of God's will and purpose. Granted, there is a time to put some things in your life to "death," many of which conflict with the purpose of God for your life. One of which is the focus on "self" as mentioned in an earlier chapter. The more we focus on Jesus, the less we are compelled to be self-centered. If more of our time was spent seeking after Him, the mysteries of God would be revealed to us. Why? Because His will for us He has purposed in

Himself (Ephesians 1:9). It is not the desire of God that we remain dead in our sins. He wants to resurrect the "inner man" and breathe new life back into him. Just as Jesus called Lazarus from the grave, He is calling us from past failures, hurts and disappointments in life in which many choose to remain. This is saddening because these are the very things that God uses to bring forth new life in us. We can either choose to revel in our failures or we can choose to put them to death and use them as stepping stones, as we are called to be the people whom God has purposed within Himself.

As believers, we are of a royal priesthood, an holy nation, a peculiar people; that we should show forth the praises of Him who has called us out of the darkness and into the marvelous light (1 Peter 2:9). Every opportunity that presents itself is an opportunity for the believer to give testimony of God's goodness and mercy.

REDEEMING THE TIME

Because our time on earth is allotted it is imperative that as believers we take advantage of every opportunity to serve God. We have been equipped with various gifts, talents and abilities to serve in extraordinary ways. The problem is that most of these attributes are often misguided in the pursuit of worldly lusts and ambitions. There's nothing wrong with wanting to achieve excellence, but the question remains — how will it benefit the Kingdom of God? That should be the question that is on every believer's mind in whatever their pursuits. How will your goals bring glory to God?

The hopes, dreams and ambitions of many Christians have taken a back seat to pain, disappointment, fear and depression, often leading to unfruitful lives; but this doesn't have to be. As mentioned earlier, the Spirit of God has resurrecting power, a power that's resident in every believer. Because the Spirit of God resides in us we have not been given a spirit of fear; but of power, and of love, and of a sound mind (II Tim. 1:7). No matter how bad a situation or circumstance may appear, God reigns supreme in the life of the believer. He says in His Word that He would restore the years that the locust have eaten (Joel 2:25). In the economy of God it's not so much how you begin the race, but whether or not you endure until the end in order to finish well.

A LIFE WELL LIVED

There are many stories that exemplify the principal of redeeming time. The Bible is filled with stories of ordinary people that no doubt had faults, but went on to live extraordinary lives. Just as their lives of faith inspire us today, there are present day lives that inspire us as well. One such story took place in rural North Carolina in a town by the name of Laurinburg. A small, yet peaceful town, it is one that is validated only by the charm of its citizens. The setting takes place in the local hospital where a dialysis patient eagerly awaits the physician's findings of his latest test results. When the doctor finally informs him of the news, the patient exhibits very little emotion, other than a small grimace, quickly recovering with a slight smile. The prognosis is not a good one, but nevertheless, the patient remains positive and upbeat. He is rooted and grounded in the Word of God, as he has been a minister of the Gospel for over twenty-two years. The news of that evening was quite bleak. As the Reverend pondered his situation, he knew in his heart that he would not be returning to the place that he had once called home. Thoughts began to enter his mind, not so much as to his condition, but more toward the welfare of his family. He was a man of conviction and fierce devotion to family. His case was unique as he was somewhat of a hometown celebrity, having lived his entire twenty-two year ministry *while undergoing dialysis treatments.* This in itself had never been heard of. He was a living example of the power of God.

As family and friends from near and far began to visit him daily, he remained confident and upbeat. He encouraged everyone that visited and reminded them that he was in God's hands. As his condition deteriorated, the presence of pain became more evident. The many years of continuous treatments, combined with his age, were beginning to take their toll. His bones were weakened over time, and the slow erosion brought about immense pain. Injections of morphine were administered to make him more comfortable, but after a while, even that began to lose its effectiveness. The now frail pastor had always been a strong man, as far as physical stature.

Twenty-two years prior to this particular evening, doctors were hovered over him in another hospital as he sank into a coma. It was one that by all indications would never allow him to regain consciousness. In fact, the doctors had given him up to die. But a miraculous thing happened that day. According to witnesses present at the time, there were two nurse's aides that entered his room and began to pray for him. They were elderly women — women of tremendous faith. They prayed for him day and night, fervently. The Scripture states that "The effectual fervent prayer of a righteous man availeth much" (James 5:16). Miraculously, within 48 hours of the diagnosis, the patient regained consciousness. He remembered everything that had taken place, but there was something *different* about him. He began to talk of being in the presence of the Almighty. He told his beloved wife Francina of a vision that he had experienced, only this seemed *real.* He told her that he had been allowed by God to see a glimpse of heaven itself. Almost impossible to believe, those who heard could not deny the vivid detail and assuredness in his description. There was an uncanny eeriness about the whole situation, but yet he spoke with such zeal. As he finished this incredible explanation of Divine intervention, he said that the Lord preserved him to come back to tell of the place which he had been allowed to see — which was heaven.

Incredible as it may seem, shortly afterwards, T.B. Ellison entered a local Bible college and was ordained as a minister of the Gospel after completing training. The following years of his ministry were characterized by an exemplary life of faith, coupled with an undying devotion to his family. The proof of his call to service was not only highlighted by his miraculous recovery and record-breaking achievements, but the obvious evidence of the "fruit of the Spirit." On April 17th 2003, after many years of service to the Lord, Reverend T.B. Ellison was called home. The later years of his life embodied the term "perseverance" for he ran the race well, and he endured to the end. In parting, he left his legacy of faith. I'm very proud to say that he was my dad. I shall miss him greatly.

My dad recognized the hand of God upon his life, even before his supernatural encounter with the Almighty. Having gone through such a life altering experience, however, prompted urgency in his spirit to spread the Gospel. For the remainder of time that God had given him, not one moment was wasted afterwards. At one time, he pastored two churches simultaneously and gave equal attention to both. He worked tirelessly to get the message out, as well as devoting time to the congregations he pastored. When his health finally began to fail, he realized the necessity to "lighten the load." In God's wisdom he came to the conclusion that he had overextended himself, and soon resigned to pastoring only one congregation. After over fifteen years of ministry, the effects of a long-term illness finally caused him to step down from the pulpit. He was no longer able to stand during the course of his sermons. He tried sitting for a while, but even that began to take a toll on him. When he finally stepped down as pastor, he contacted a local radio station and began to record radio sermons on weekends to honor his commitment to the Lord. When he could no longer travel to the station, my mother delivered his tapes to the station. They were pre-recorded in the privacy of their home, but not one ounce of passion or love of God's Word was spared in his recordings. Is it any wonder why God extended his years far beyond the initial prognosis? God had a plan for my father, just as He has a plan for you and me as believers.

Dad found his purpose in the pursuit of the Kingdom. He realized that his purpose had been wrapped up in Jesus all along. When He discovered that, he performed the miraculous. In doing so, many were able to witness as to what God can do, if you are willing to let Him take control of your life. Isaiah 40 v. 31 bears witness to this in saying, "But they that wait upon the Lord shall renew their strength; they shall mount up with wings as eagles; they shall run, and not be weary; and they shall walk, and not faint." Yes, my father waited on the Lord many times throughout the remainder of his life. Each and every time he was strengthened far beyond expectations. His rallying cry came out of James 5 v. 15, "And the prayer of faith shall save the sick, and the Lord shall raise him up; and if he have committed sins, they shall be forgiven him." He put "substance" behind his faith. Both he and those who trusted and believed God for a miracle received it according to their faith. The difference was in knowing what the Word of God "stated" as opposed to what the circumstances "dictated." Neither he nor my mother pondered the question, "Hath God said?" They *knew* the promises of God and *acted* upon them. Because of that, both were able to give God glory.

After all, isn't that what this life is all about? Have we not been created to glorify God? When we face adversity and apply God's principles, we exalt Jesus in the process. We give testimony of everything that He accomplished on the Cross by walking in the victory that He has already provided. It's not always easy, but God has given us the grace by which to persevere, and the promise that He will be with us in the process (Deuteronomy 4:31). Because of the seeds of faith that were so diligently sown over the course of my father's life the harvest of faith flows in abundance in our family. In viewing his example in regards to relationship to our Heavenly Father, we were strengthened in our walk. By never giving up, never giving in to his circumstances, Reverend T.B. Ellison became a beacon of light for those on the verge of despair, a voice of hope in the wilderness of Jesus' gift of redemption, salvation, restoration, and the miraculous sustaining power of the Almighty God.

Now that we know that our time has been allotted, how do we as Christians make the most of it? God has gifted all of us in one way or another. The gifting is for service. As we honor God with our gifts, He will honor us with His favor. We are called to be good stewards of the manifold grace of God (I Peter 4:10), and that includes the stewardship of our *time.*

CHAPTER SEVEN

THE IMPORTANCE OF PRAYER

"Be careful for nothing; but in everything by prayer and supplication with thanksgiving let your requests be made known unto God." (Philippians 4:6)

Of the many spiritual disciplines, perhaps the most effective is the discipline of prayer. Prayer is the key to unlocking the mysteries of the Kingdom of God. When exercised, prayer can be the single most effective weapon in the believer's arsenal of spiritual warfare. First of all, what is prayer? Prayer, simply defined, is communication with God. Just as human beings communicate with one another through conversation, prayer is the means by which we communicate with God. When Christ was on the earth, He was in constant communication with God, the Father. In doing so, He modeled humility, dependence upon the Father, submission and relationship. Often, Jesus would isolate Himself from everyone in order to be alone with the Father. This allowed Him to focus directly on the will of the Father.

JESUS, OUR HIGH PRIEST

Jesus intentionally avoided the crowds of people at times, and occasionally, even His apostles. But this was all for good reason, as much as His Deity was evident, He was at the same time, fully human. As a man, He experienced human emotions such as sorrow (Matthew 26:38), agony (Luke 22:44), and grief (Mark 3:5). In His humanity, Jesus also required sleep. This was necessary to rejuvenate His physical body. Mark 4 v. 38 describes Jesus as being in the furthermost part of a ship sleeping on a pillow. The fact that He had a pillow is a good indication that His sleep was intentional. All of these attributes help to substantiate Jesus' humanity.

In light of these facts, recent times find us in the midst of heretical teachings concerning the humanity of Christ. There are those that would have us to believe that Christ was just a man, like any other man, but this is simply not true. Despite his humanity, He was – and still is – fully God. He is in fact, God incarnate. His miraculous birth and sinless life attest to His Deity. He is the Son of God, the One who was with God in the beginning. "In the beginning was the Word and the Word was with God, and the Word was God" (John 1:1). He needed no "special" anointing because He Himself being the *Logos*, or Word of God, *became* flesh to dwell amongst His creation (John 1:14).

Jesus is the Heir of all things, the express image of the Father, and upholds everything by the word of His power (Hebrews 1: 2-3). Isaiah 9 v. 6 refers to Jesus as "The mighty God," the "Everlasting Father." According to Colossians 2 v. 9, all the fullness of the Godhead dwells within Him. Titus 2 v. 13 refers to Jesus as "Great God." He is the great "I Am" in John 8:58, and "Lord God Almighty" in Revelation 4 v. 8. The reason for the incarnation was two-fold. First of all, Jesus came to seek and save the lost. The second and most compelling reason was to become the living sacrifice for the remission of sin. Scripture teaches, there is no remission of sins without the shedding of blood (Hebrews 9:22). Throughout the Old Testament, the blood of the innocent was shed for the transgressions of the guilty. Jesus became the ultimate sacrifice for all of mankind. In the Old Testament, the high priest brought animal sacrifices before God on behalf of the people. He was designated to come into the presence of God to make intercession for the sins of the people. Today, this is no longer necessary because these were only ceremonies that foreshadowed what Jesus was to do upon the Cross for all of mankind. The innocent, sinless blood of the Lamb of God was shed for the remission of sin. His sacrifice "pleased" the Father (Isaiah 53:10), and because of it we are able to come into the presence of God on our own. Jesus' humanity and subsequent sacrifice of Himself uniquely qualifies Him to be our Advocate, our High Priest.

PRAYER DEVELOPS RELATIONSHIP

The one necessity in any human relationship is communication. Without communication there can be no relationship. Communication opens up avenues of discussion that often lead to understanding the way a person thinks, feels, and general outlook on life. It is a means by which we relate to one another. Prayer is how we communicate with God. By spending time with Him in prayer and meditating in His Word, we form a personal relationship with Him. It is the will of God that we come to know Him as our Heavenly Father. The Bible itself is God's revelation to us as to who He is. Romans 8 v. 15 says that we receive the "Spirit of adoption" whereby we cry "Abba Father." Isn't it interesting that one of the first utterances that a newborn baby makes sounds like the word "Abba"? When we accept Jesus as Lord, our Heavenly Father sees us as His children. As His children, we can relate to Him according to our adoption status. So, just how does prayer develop relationship with God?

First of all, the more time you spend with God, the more you get to know Him. The same could be said in reference to earthly relationships. The more time you spend with someone, the more you become acquainted with their habits, thoughts, goals and desires. Just as a parent has goals and desires for their children, God has purposed certain goals and desires for us as well. How do we know this? God Himself expresses His thoughts in Jeremiah 29 v. 11 in saying, "For I know the thoughts that I think toward you, thoughts of peace, and not of evil, to give you an expected end." David expounds concerning the thoughts of God in saying, "If I should count them, they are more in number than the sand: when awake, I am still with thee" (Psalms 139:18). It is also God's desire that all would come to salvation and the knowledge of the truth (I Timothy 2:4).

Scripture also tells us that His thoughts are higher than our thoughts. Because His thoughts of us are higher God sees us in a much different light than we see ourselves. He views us in light of who He created us to be and not so much as to who we appear to be. God is patient throughout the sanctification process because certain "discrepancies" must be worked out in order to be conformed to the image of His Son. This often requires prayer. As we face difficulties in life, sometimes driving us to the innermost recesses of pain and despair, there arises a need to cry out, "Abba Father"; the hurt being so severe, that only the soothing hand of God can relieve it. Pain is uncomfortable and sometimes unrelenting, but yet there are times when it becomes necessary to drive us to the throne of God. By no means does He desire to "force" Himself upon anyone, as He has given us all free will. But His desire is that we grow in dependence on Him. He wants us to rely on Him for all of our needs. It is interesting to note that in the context of a family environment even the most stubborn of children come to conformity, given the right circumstances. If a child is disobedient, and the result initiates pain and suffering, eventually that child will recognize the "source" of that pain and come to repentance. But who does the child come to in order to ease the pain — to "make things right"? Most often to the parent. The reason that the child comes to the parent essentially revolves around relationship.

The same principle applies to us as adults. Even the most independent, self-reliant individual will "learn" to come to God in prayer, given the right circumstances. They may not have a personal relationship with God, but yet they will call on Him in times of distress. When catastrophes strike, such as floods, earthquakes, hurricanes or drought, people will pray. Sadly, far too many Christians seek God *only* in times of difficulty. We must seek the Lord while He may be found, call upon Him while He is near (Isaiah 55:6). He is interested in everything that concerns us, and wants to be involved in every aspect of our lives.

HOW MUST WE PRAY?

When we pray, we are to pray to the Father in secret; Jesus explains in Matthew 6 v. 6. We do so that we may be rewarded openly by God in light of our petition. We are discouraged from making vain repetitions (Matthew 6:7) and extensive prayer because God already knows the need (Matthew 6:8). He looks upon the heart, whereby the Holy Spirit searches the intent of the heart. Many prayers are sent up with the wrong intent or motivation. Prayer is based on an "attitude of gratitude," and what you *feel* will most often reflect *how* you pray. There are some that pray openly before others that they may receive "accolades" for eloquence of speech. This type of praying does not impress God because it does not exude the right motive. If your motive for prayer is to impress others, according to Scripture, you have already received your reward (Matthew 6:5). So how then, must we pray?

First of all, we must recognize who God is, in respect to His holiness, character, and sovereignty. Jesus instructed His disciples on how to pray in His model prayer in Matthew 6 vv. 9-13. He begins with "Our Father, who art in heaven, hallowed be thy name." The word "hallowed" in the Greek means "holy." So God must be recognized as holy. The word "Father," in light of the text, makes reference to God as "parent" to His children. So, in the beginning of this model prayer God's sovereignty and holiness is established. The next phrase projects, "Thy kingdom come, thy will be done in earth as it is in heaven." This is a petition for the Kingdom of God to be established here in the earth realm, just as it has already been established in heaven. It is a request for the merger of the "unseen" things of God, which are located in heavenly places to be made manifest within the earthly realm. Since the kingdom of heaven operates under the sovereign and righteous authority of God, His perfect will creates perfect peace, a harmonious atmosphere. This is one of the reasons why Scripture directs us to pray for those who are in authority over us, so that we may lead quiet, peaceful, and godly lives (I Timothy 2:12). Also contained in Jesus' prayer is the understanding that God is our provider. All provision comes from Him. He is our very source of existence. Since He created us, He knows exactly what it takes to sustain us. The passage reads, "Give us this day, our daily bread." Our daily bread is a reflection of the "manna" that God provided for the children of Israel while crossing through the wilderness. God today, just as He did back then, still provides for His children. For those who believe on His Son and trust in Him, He meets the needs of those who find themselves in the wilderness, in a "dry" place. In Christ, there is no lack of provision because God the Father has purposed everything in Him.

Christ also models *forgiveness* in His prayer. Without forgiveness we would be completely lost and dead in our sins. In the presence of a holy and righteous God, in our own righteousness, we are as filthy rags before Him (Isaiah 64:6). We are non-deserving of His grace and mercy because of sin. But under the blood of Jesus, we are clothed in His *righteousness*. He alone is worthy because He has paid the sin "debt" in full. This is why we can come before the throne of God saying "And forgive us our debts, as we forgive our debtors." Because we are covered by the blood of Jesus, we have been "justified" in order to come before our Heavenly Father, in the righteousness of His Son, to ask for forgiveness based on what He has already done. Because we have been forgiven He expects us to forgive others in return. Peter asked Jesus "Lord, how often shall my brother sin against me and I forgive him? till seven times?" Jesus replied, "I say not unto thee, until seven times: but, until seventy times seven." The point that Jesus was trying to make to Peter was that the number of times to forgive wasn't the real issue, but rather the *willingness* to forgive is what sets the precedent.

PRAY FERVENTLY

What is fervent prayer? It is an intense, yet passionate petition to God for His Divine intervention on behalf of your circumstance. Fervent prayer is heated prayer. Oftentimes, it is born out of desperation and fueled by intensity. It comes from deep within the heart out of the lowest recesses of one's belly, crying out to God; your soul laid bare before him. A fervent prayer comes in many variations. For some it comes in the way of weeping and moaning before God in anguish and despair. For others it may come as a shout or a dance in praise for who He is. And yet it may come in the form of those who lay prostrate before God, as David did in reverence to His holiness. Whichever way it comes, praying with fervency gets God's attention. James said it best when he said, "The effectual fervent prayer of a righteous man availeth much." God responds to a fervent prayer because it usually comes with no "hidden agenda." The plea is usually one of urgency and complete dependency upon Him.

When a mother hears the cry of her child, she naturally responds to the needs of that child. But if she should hear that same child "scream," then the normal response is intensified! The scream is an indication of "abnormality" and a sense of urgency is detected. When we fervently pray to God, He detects our sense of urgency. Of course, He knows of our needs before we petition Him, but because He sees the heart the intensity of prayer is a reflection of what's contained inside of the heart. And just as a mother responds to the screams of her child, God responds to our fervent prayer.

PRAY FREQUENTLY

I Thessalonians 5 v. 17 charges us to "pray without ceasing." When we think of prayer, we often think of being on our knees before God with head bowed and hands clasped in order to worship Him properly. While this is an honorable way to worship God, it is by no means the only way to pray to Him. Since prayer is "communication" with God and we are told to "pray without ceasing," difficulties would surely arise if we confined the act of prayer to one particular posture. While praying on bended knee is an act of submission and reverence to God, He is more concerned with the posture of the heart.

Prayer takes place when our thoughts are "linked" to God's Word. While meditating on His Word and thinking of the truths within it, we in essence are praying to God. Paul says in Philippians 4 v. 8, "Finally, brethren, whatsoever things are true, whatsoever things are honest, whatsoever things are just, whatsoever things are pure, whatsoever things are lovely, whatsoever things are of good report; if there be any virtue, and if there be any praise, think on these things." Although prayer is an action, it is a deliberate action, a mindset, one that is designed to seek and attain the attention of God. Because God knows our thoughts if we are thinking on the good things that Paul described, we are in communication with God.

PRAY WITH PERSISTENCE

How many times have you given up on something just before the breakthrough came? You think to yourself "If only I would have just hung in there for a little while longer, I would have reaped the harvest." It happens to people all of the time. It happens to the student who fails the big exam for lack of study or the athlete that falls short of his or her intended goal due to lack of practice or motivation. It even happens in the home to the parent that at some point decides that he's had enough and tragically walks out of the lives of his children. In each case there is a lack of commitment and persistence.

Prayer takes a great deal of commitment, as well as persistence. It's not an easy task, as there are many distractions that compete for our attention. But regardless of the detractors, we must be persistent if we want to see results in our prayer lives. Nothing good is ever attained by giving up; so when we seek God, we must pray, and pray without ceasing. Sometimes it may seem that nothing is happening, that it's all just a waste of time. Be assured, if you are a child of God, your Heavenly Father hears your cry; and as you wait on Him, He will answer. You may not always receive the answer you expect nor will it always come in the way you expect it; but nevertheless, it will come.

Daniel was persistent in his prayer. Scripture says that God heard his prayer from the very first day (Daniel 10:12), but there was an interruption of twenty-one days that was caused by demonic intervention. This interruption caused a three week delay in the answer to Daniel's prayer. When the answer finally came, the messenger fitted Daniel with an explanation. The backdrop of the explanation paints a vivid picture of spiritual warfare: the angelic messengers of the Most High, engaging demonic forces in spiritual conflict, on behalf of the saints! This ever intensified struggle is happening daily, in the lives of all saints.

This is all the more reason why prayer must be persistent. Heaven must be petitioned frequently if for no other reason that God may send "assistance" to your answer. In the case of Daniel, God sent the archangel, Michael to aid in the release of Daniel's answer (Daniel 10:13). Until this time, Daniel mourned and fasted. Sometimes, when we seek to hear from God, there must be a willingness to sacrifice, a willingness to do whatever it takes to get our answer. First of all, we must be willing to *ask* God for what we want or need. Then we must *seek* Him diligently *expecting* a response. Why the expectancy? His character — because He is true to His Word God will do as He says. "They shall call on my name, and I will hear them: I will say, It is my people: and they shall say, The Lord is my God" (Zechariah 13:9). Yes, God does indeed hear the cries of His people, and when we call upon Him, we have His Word that He will answer.

HEAVENLY ACCESS

Prayer gives us access to heaven. Now, Jesus is Lord over all of creation because all power has been given to Him in all of heaven and earth (Matthew 28:18). Even now, He sits on the right hand of the Father making intercession for the saints (Romans 8:34). Because of His finished work on Calvary we as believers have been given a position of authority through prayer. Although Christ is our High Priest, we have been made priest alongside Him. While here on the earth as a man, Jesus had access to whatever He needed to accomplish the will of the Father. He had access to the angelic hosts as described in Matthew 26 v. 53 saying, "Thinkest thou that I cannot pray to my Father, and He shall presently give me more than twelve legions of angels?" Jesus could have done so at any time, had He needed them. It is important to note that the method for His request would have been through prayer.

When we are in need of anything, we have only but to pray and our Heavenly Father hears us. His angels are ministering spirits that assist in carrying out His will. Just as Daniel awaited his answer, and our Lord could have summoned legions of angels at His disposal, they minister to us as well. Prayer is the catalyst that sets things in motion, the means by which God is prompted to move on our behalf. It is one of the most effective means of confronting chaos. It was prayer that enabled the servant of Elisha, the prophet of God, to access heaven. Scripture describes how Elisha and his servant arose early one morning, only to find themselves completely surrounded by soldiers of the Syrian army. Having been sent by their king to arrest Elisha, they were great in number. The servant of Elisha panicked saying, "Alas master! How shall we do?" Elisha answered, "Fear not: for they that be with us are more than they that be with them." (II Kings 6:15- 16)." You see, Elisha saw something that his servant could not see at the time. He saw the heavenly army that the Lord had sent on his behalf. Scripture says that Elisha prayed that his servant's eyes be opened that he might be able to see as he did. "And the Lord opened the eyes of the young man; and he saw: and, behold, the mountain was full of horses and chariots of fire round about Elisha" (II Kings 6:17). When we pray according to the will of God, He dispatches his angels to accomplish His will and to serve His purpose. Since God doesn't change, He will do just as He did with Elisha. The key is communication with Him, and prayer is the catalyst to heavenly access.

Peter and John witnessed to the masses in Acts chapter 4. Scripture denotes, "And when they had prayed, the place was shaken where they were assembled together; and they were all filled with the Holy Ghost, and they spake the word of God with boldness" (Acts 4:31). Prayer gave them access to heaven, and supernatural power and authority came about as a result. Paul and Silas witnessed that same power in Acts 16:26. After praying and singing praises to God, while locked away in a prison, Scripture recalls that there came a great "earthquake" that "shook" the foundations of the prison, and immediately all the doors were opened, and everyone's bands were loosed. What a powerful representation of the power of prayer. The prison that held Paul and Silas could very well be symbolic of spiritual strongholds that hinder our growth in Christ. Prayer and praise were the catalyst that accessed heaven and loosed them from their bondage. In the midst of our struggle our pain, and sometimes fear, it is good to remember that we serve a God that will never leave nor forsake us. Paul and Silas worshiped Him for who He is. They did not allow their circumstance to steal their joy. Instead, they rose above it and focused solely on the worship of Almighty God.

One can only speculate as to the content of such prayer that would be so powerful as to cause God to move in such a spectacular fashion. Yes, heaven is accessible while yet here on earth. God wants us to seek Him when we are in need. He wants us to cry out to Him when we are "pressed out of measure." The same angelic hosts that he sent to aid Elisha, Daniel, and Paul and Silas are waiting to aid us in this struggle in which we find ourselves. Remember, "For we wrestle not against flesh and blood, but against principalities, against powers, against the rulers of the darkness of this world, against spiritual wickedness in high places" (Ephesians 6:12). Because we wrestle against spiritual wickedness in high places, we need to have access to "high places." The only way to access these places are through prayer. We must also remember that our High Priest, our Advocate, resides in heavenly places. He is our Lord, Jesus Christ, who is continually making intercession for the saints.

PRAYER ALIGNS US WITH GOD

As we pray, focusing on God's attributes and character, it is very easy to marvel at the splendor of His majesty. So awesome is the essence of His being that we recognize ourselves for who we are, just as Isaiah did, as he replied, "But we are all as an unclean thing, and all our righteousness are as filthy rags; and we all do fade as a leaf; and our iniquities, like the wind, have taken us away" (Isaiah 64:6). Isaiah knew that once he was in the presence of a holy God, that he was inadequate. In all of his righteousness, he could not begin to compare to the righteousness of God. "Woe is me! for I am undone," Isaiah cries out in Isaiah 6 v. 5 "Because I am a man of unclean lips, and I dwell in the midst of a people of unclean lips: for mine eyes have seen the King, the Lord of hosts."

Have you felt the presence of the Lord of hosts in your prayer life? When you pray, do you focus on the character and attributes of Almighty God? Do you recognize Him as Lord over your life, and do you recognize Him as the life-giver? If so, then your prayers are most likely fervent and effective. As we bow in the presence of the Most High God, we are forced to "come clean" with our true state. We can only stand before Him in the righteousness of His Son, whom was sent that we might be redeemed. Only by his blood are we cleansed of our iniquities and purged of our sins. When we come to that realization, then we can be used by God to reach others who are in need of a Savior.

PRAY GOD'S WORD

One of the most effective means of prayer is to pray the Word of God. As we learn the Word, and as it becomes a part of who we are, we begin to walk in the spirit. As we learn to walk in the spirit, our prayer life will undergo a transformation of sorts to where it becomes almost second nature to automatically pray in relationship to God's Word. As we are transformed by the renewing of our minds (by reading and meditating on Scripture), we develop the "Mind of Christ." Paul referred to the mind of Christ in I Corinthians 2 v. 16. The meaning here implies that one that has the mind of Christ is one that is *spiritually* minded. In other words, the Spirit of God dwells within them and they are led to do the will of God.

So, how do we pray God's Word? The first thing we must do is to *study* His Word, so that we show ourselves approved unto God, workmen that need not be ashamed, but rightfully dividing the Word of truth (II Timothy 2:15). When we know what the Word of God states, we are better able to articulate His Word back to Him in a manner to where it holds God "accountable" to what He has said. That's right, "accountable." You may be thinking "But who are we, to hold God accountable for anything?" It's not we who hold God accountable, but His "Word." You see, as we pray according to God's purpose, He responds because He honors His Word above His name (Psalms 138:2). As we are led by the Spirit of God, and as we develop the mind of Christ, we learn to pray in relation to the will of God according to His Word and that opens up the windows of heaven, allowing us to experience the miraculous.

CHAPTER EIGHT

THE PLANTING SEASON

"While the earth remaineth, seedtime and harvest, and cold and heat, and summer and winter, and day and night shall not cease." (Genesis 8:22)

As long as the earth has been in existence, the spiritual law of seedtime and harvest has been in effect. When God created the earth, He created it establishing this law whereby everything that was created would produce *seed* of its own kind. From the herbs of the field to man himself, everything that was given life has the potential to reproduce of its own likeness. The word "seed" is mentioned many times throughout the Bible and is usually used in conjunction with sowing or "planting." Jesus elaborates on the principle of sowing and reaping in Mark chapter 4, when He illustrates the parable of the sower. He describes different scenarios pertaining to the sowing process and the disruptions that hinder the seed from being firmly planted into the soil. The parable is used as an illustration as to how the Word of God is sometimes "choked off," and never reaches the fertile soil of the heart.

When a farmer sows seed in a field, the expectation is that the seed will produce the product that it represents. For instance, if the desired product happened to be apples, then apple seeds would need to be sown, and if the desired product happened to be wheat, then the seed for wheat would have to been sown. Once planted, and if sown properly, with reasonable irrigation and sunlight, the seed germinates, and begins its reproductive process. The same holds true with the Word of God.

Jesus refers to the "seed" as being the "Word" in Mark chapter 4, and the sower of the seed, the believer. As the Word is spoken or *sown*, it carries the potential to produce whatever is contained in it, according to the will of God, as it is received. Jesus said in Mark 4 v. 9, "He that hath ears to hear, let him hear." So, it is important to "hear" the Word in order for it to "take root." Why? Again, because faith comes by hearing, and hearing by the Word of God (Romans 10:17).

You may ask, "What role does faith have to play in this process?" The answer: Plenty. You see, in order for seed to take root, it has to be planted in fertile soil. The soil in Jesus' illustration refers to the heart of man. Once the "seed," or "Word" goes forth, "faith" *cultivates* the heart in order to receive it. Once it takes root, the continuous "hearing" of the Word is what waters it. The apostle Paul was aware of this spiritual law, and in I Corinthians 3 v. 6 made this statement: "I have planted, Apollos watered; but God gave the increase." Sometimes, all we can do is to plant the seed. In other words, "tell" someone about Jesus. It may take someone else to come along, just as Apollos did in Paul's case, to expound on what had already been spoken. Newly planted seed cannot be expected to take root immediately. It takes time to germinate. In most cases, it must be watered.

WATERING YOUR FIELD

As Christians, we should be doing either one of two things. In responding to the Great Commission that Christ gave the church, we should be planting seed; that is, spreading the Gospel of Jesus Christ, or we should be watering the seed. It is important to note however, that even though we plant and water, only God can bring the increase. Once we have witnessed to others of the Gospel, it is up to the Holy Spirit to illuminate and lead to Salvation. As we are inspired by the Word of God, and led by His Spirit, the planting and watering process should flow from a sense of gratitude, a thankful heart; one that seeks only to please God. There should be an ever present visibility of the Holy Spirit at work in every believer. That visible, tangible evidence should bear "fruit" of good works; that first being love, joy, peace, longsuffering, gentleness, goodness, faith, meekness, and temperance (Galatians 5:22,23). Unknowingly to some Christians however, these attributes reflect the character of our Heavenly Father, and in many cases serve as the "irrigation" mechanism for the "dry" seed or the weary soul. Sometimes there are circumstances where someone has already heard the Word, but hesitate to commit to what it says; the reason being for lack of faith or unbelief. The absolute best witness that we as Christians can give, outside of our verbal testimony, is the visible example of how we live. It's the tangible acts of exhibiting God's love toward one another, bearing one another's burdens and exalting the name of Jesus that draws attention; that "irrigates" the field. As we have been filled with "springs of living water," knowing that it is Christ who lives in us, we should exude extreme confidence in knowing that it is He who empowers us, both to will and to do the purposes of God. As Christ offered the abundance of life to the Samaritan woman at the well, we in turn have also received and accepted that same gift. His words to her in John 4 vs. 14 were, "But whosoever drinketh of the water that I shall give him shall never thirst; but the water that I shall give him shall be in him a well of water springing up into everlasting life."

As we are followers of the Lord Jesus Christ, having been filled with the Holy Spirit, and saved by the grace of God, we possess the capacity to "water" the seed as opportunities present themselves to us. The dry seed is not hard to find. We have only but to look around us. It has been scattered throughout the earth. We find dry seed in our families, our neighborhoods, workplaces, and governments. In virtually every walk of life, there is dry seed that requires the "stimulus" of the "living" water of the Lord Jesus Christ. As we water our fields, God will most certainly bring increase to His Word. In the process, hearts will be mended, strongholds will be broken, sorrow and sickness will cease to be an impediment to the abundant joy that is found in Christ. Of course, there will be trials, difficulties in life that continue to challenge the promises of God. The question of "Hath God said," will frequently come to mind in the midst of difficult circumstances. But when God brings the increase, the fruit of perseverance and patience, combined with prayer and supplication, will help you to rise above those difficulties, and bring you to a place of "rest" in the Lord. There is a constant need for watering because there is such a tremendous field. With that being the case, we are to pray for more laborers because the harvest is plentiful but the laborers are few (Matthew 9:37). By watering the dry seed, we not only fulfill the will of God to be effective witnesses for the kingdom, but we also serve in advancing the Kingdom of God.

THE FIELD OF THORNS

There are many things that get in the way of the sower and the proper planting of the seed. One of those obstacles happens to be the presence of thorns in the field. Jesus illustrates this in Mark chapter 4 as He describes the thorns that grow up in the field, eventually "choking" the seed to the point that it can bear no fruit. There are thorns that "choke" the Word before it can take root in the heart. They have to do with the cares of this world, the restless pace in which we live. Because we live in a post-modern culture there are many distractions that compete for our attention. The less attentive we are to the Word, the greater the chances that it will not be able to take root. And if it doesn't take root, then what? Well, because it contains the will of God for our lives, chances are, we stand to miss out on a great deal of the abundant life that God has promised for the believer. With the advent of modern electronics and such an array of high-tech "gadgetry," it is becoming more difficult to spend "quiet time" with God.

Sometimes we have to "break away" from these distractions so that we can hear from our Creator, to listen to His instruction, His plan as to how we should live. After all, isn't He the One that drew up the blueprints in the first place? When we neglect to seek after Him, to listen for His voice, we open ourselves up to chaos. It's comparable to a ship at sea without the benefit of a compass, or a plane full of passengers at thirty thousand feet without the benefit of a pilot. There's no way of knowing where you are heading, no sense of direction or stability.

The distractions of this world can lead us to worry, thereby "choking off" the Word to the point that it is of "non-effect" if it is not allowed to take root. In Luke 12 v. 25 Jesus said, "And which of you with taking thought can add to his stature one cubit?" He was referring to the sin of "worry."

Yes, worrying is a sin, because it reflects unbelief. It exhibits a lack of faith in the promises of God. If His Word is allowed to take root in the heart, as it is watered, it will begin to increase. As the increase comes, there will be less room left for worry. As worry begins to fade, doubt and fear have no basis on which to stand. They are the offspring of worrying. We must be careful to remove the thorns from our field, so that the seed can take proper root!

Along with the fast pace of life and all of its busyness comes the temptation of riches and the lusts of other things. Jesus describes this in Mark 4 v. 19 saying, "And the cares of this world, and the deceitfulness of riches, and the lusts of other things entering in, choke the Word, and it becometh unfruitful." Again, the Word is of non-effect when we allow vanity and deception to replace the will of God. We must guard against the pursuit of vanity. According to Psalms 24 v. 1, "The earth is the Lord's and the fullness thereof; the world, and they that dwell therein." Do we not dwell in this world, created by Almighty God? As sure as this is true, then that means we belong to Him. We are as seeds scattered throughout the earth in representation of God's rule and dominion here on the earth. As we are led by His Spirit and "fed" by His Word, we grow in spirit and begin to "produce" according to our faith and knowledge of the Word. Jesus spoke of the various increments of return based on receiving the Word. He said in Mark 4 v. 20, "And these are they which are sown on good ground; such as hear the Word, and receive it, and bring forth fruit, some thirtyfold, some sixty, and some an hundred." According to this passage, the "yielding" potential of the believer is based on the "hearing" of the Word and how it is received. As it is heard and acted upon, then transformation will begin to take place.

God said, "So shall my Word be that goeth forth out of my mouth: it shall not return unto me void, but it shall accomplish that which I please, and it shall prosper in the thing whereto I sent it" (Isaiah 55:11). Knowing that God is true to His Word, we should also take comfort in the knowledge that contained in it is the potential for living a victorious life. Many Christians are living in defeat for their lack of knowledge and their "unwillingness" to "act" on the Word of God. "If any man have ears to hear, let him hear," are the words of Jesus in Mark 4 v. 23. As we are receptive to the Word, God will reveal spiritual truths that will in turn bring increase into our lives. We first have to be "teachable" in order for the Word to have effect. "Take heed what ye hear: with what measure ye mete, it shall be measured to you: and unto you that hear shall more be given" (Mark 4:24). As you hear the Word and respond to it, your receptiveness will determine how much more will be revealed to you. To those that receive it, the thirty, sixty, and sometimes one-hundred fold harvest gives glory to God. These are the saints that take God at His Word and bring forth "fruit."

Remember, God said that His Word would not return to Him void, but would prosper in the thing whereto He sends it. For those who are not bearing fruit, who have difficulty in producing the thirty fold, sixty, and even one-hundred fold harvest there are several reasons. They are either not hearing the Word, not acting upon the Word, or it is being *taken away.*

THE STOLEN WORD

Whenever a farmer plants seed in the field, there are those seeds that fail to penetrate the soil. For those that do so and remain scattered on top of the soil, the likelihood of being "snatched away" by the birds or *fowls of the air* is greatly increased. The potential is there because of the exposure of the seed. In order for the seed to germinate or take root, it has to be planted deep into the soil. If you, as a believer, hear the Word but fail to keep it in your heart, you run the risk at having it stolen from you. You may ask, "How is this possible?" Jesus gives us an example in Mark 4 v. 15 when He states, "And these are they by the way side, where the Word is sown; but when they have heard, Satan cometh *immediately*, and taketh away the Word that was sown in their hearts."

Now, Scripturally speaking, Satan is also known as the "prince of the power of the air." Just as the birds "snatch" the exposed seed, Satan snatches the exposed Word. It is not at all uncommon for a Christian, after just attending church services, to "forget" most of what he has just heard. In most cases, it doesn't take much for Satan to steal the Word. He may come in the form of a motorist who inadvertently "cuts you off" while exiting the parking lot. If this action provokes you to lose your temper, then Satan has successfully stolen the Word from you! Remember, the Word says that He comes immediately to take away the Word that's sown in our hearts. He will come disguised in ways that we may not easily detect, which is all the more reason to be ever vigilant. He sometimes comes by way of our children, and upon hearing the Word, your child may do or say something that causes you to respond in a derogatory manner. If this happens, then Satan has effectively stolen the Word from you. Any action or response that is outside of the will of God reflects the inability of the seed to take root. If you are a Christian, just as surely as you are exposed to the Word, expect Satan to show up at any time in an attempt to take it away!

STONES HINDER GROWTH

In the farmer's field there are sometimes stones that hinder the growth of the crops. Unless these stones are removed, the yielding potential may be reduced. There are those that hear the Word and receive it with gladness, as Jesus explains in v. 16 of Mark, chapter 4. But when adversity comes, when trouble shows up at their doorstep, they are lacking in response to the trouble. The Word is not being used as a foundation on which to stand. These are the Christians that resort to carnal responses for spiritual problems. Most often they will exhibit signs of anxiety and fear for lack of knowledge of the Word. It has become as "non-effect" in their lives because of unbelief. As mentioned earlier, there are those that "talk the talk" but fail to "walk the walk." If the seed has not been allowed to penetrate your heart to where your response is anything less than a godly one, then your seed has fallen upon "stony" ground. Chances are you have not allowed it to penetrate the depths of your heart. If you find yourself wanting to "retreat" at the first sign of trouble, something is wrong. There is a "blockage" that needs to be removed so that the Word of God can be allowed to do that thing for what He has sent it to do. Verse 17 in the same chapter of Mark reads, "And have no root in themselves, and so endure but for a time: afterward, when affliction or persecution ariseth for the Word's sake, immediately they are offended." Again, these are seeds that have not been allowed to become embedded in the soil. They have not been allowed to take root and can only endure but for a time before they are rendered ineffective.

Have you allowed the Word to become ineffective in your life? Do you receive the Word with gladness on Sunday, and yet on Monday you become the person in your home or office to avoid? If so, perhaps it's time for a personal evaluation. Perhaps the Word has not been allowed to take root. Once planted, and if properly rooted, it should produce positive results. Because the seed is of God everything contained in it should exhibit *traits* of His character. People should be drawn to those characteristics as they are life-giving in nature. They are traits that compel people to ask, "Where did you come from?" or "How can I get what you have?" As believers, we are to "attract" because of what's inside of us.

Because we carry the seed of God, which is His Word, it will produce a positive effect on those around us, allowing us to be effective witnesses for the Kingdom of God. If the stones are not removed however, our witness is affected. We can be limited based on our "taking in" of the Word. As Scripture states, there are some that will produce thirty-fold, sixty-fold, and one-hundred fold. It all depends on what type of soil the seed is planted.

FERTILE GROUND

Fertile ground is considered to be rich in nutrients and ideal for planting. It has the potential for producing a "bumper" crop, in terms of earthly standards. Spiritually speaking, when the "heart" is right, we become more receptive to the Word. We become "teachable" and are more apt to apply what we hear. The fertile soil is cultivated through trials and adversity, and is fortified by the witness of other saints. They testify of the truth of God and the faithfulness to follow through on the promises of His Word. This, coupled with one's own personal witness of the ability of God to perform the miraculous, help to build faith. These are the elements that come together to produce the fertile ground for the planting of God's Word.

It was David who said, "Create in me a clean heart, O God; and renew a right spirit within me" (Psalms 51:10). What was the reason for this request? David knew that a clean heart is fertile soil for the Word of God to penetrate. David certainly had enough trouble in his life to last us all a lifetime, but despite it all he was known as "A man after God's own heart." Why was that? Because despite the disparity and adversity that plagued him, David continuously kept God at the forefront of his life. He did not allow chaos to overrule his destiny. In Psalms 16:8 David expounds, "I have set the Lord always before me: because he is at my right hand, I shall not be moved." The fertile soil in which the seed had taken root produced the effect that God intended it to produce. David brought forth the one-hundred fold harvest as he continuously kept God before Him. As a man after God's own heart, his life was one that drew others to God. It served as a "magnet" of sorts, in the example of what God can do when the heart is "right." In his youth, David found himself face to face with both a lion and a bear. These were "stepping stones" as to where God was taking him, nutrients to be placed in the soil of the heart. Although physically, they were seen as beasts, but spiritually they represented adversity. With each and every victory that's won there is a building of faith, faith in the God that sustains you, faith that the same God will be there for you no matter what.

Is your soil fertile? Are the nutrients in your soil right for the planting? Have you been tested through fiery trials and witnessed the mercy of God? If so, then your soil is conditioned for the hundred-fold harvest. More than likely, you are receptive to the seed. If you hunger after the Word of God, and your thoughts are set on the things of God, then like David, you have placed God continuously before you. Because a clean heart has been created in you the conditions are prime for a "bumper" crop. There will be evidence of the seed "taking root" as you exhibit traits of the character of the One who sent His Word for the abundance of your life.

Remember, as believers we all are a part of the Vine. As Jesus is the Vine and we are the branches; as we grow, we will begin to take on His traits and characteristics. He said in John 15:5, "I am the vine, ye are the branches: He that abideth in me, and I in him, the same bringeth forth much fruit: for without me ye can do nothing." As long as we abide in Christ, we can be fruitful; but Jesus makes it clear, if we choose not to abide in Him, eventually we wither and die. As the storms of life come, if we are not firmly rooted in the Word of God, trials and adversity will cause us to wither on the Vine, which will in turn lead to being "cast away" and "burned" as described in John 15:6. Therefore, it behooves us as Christians to stay attached to the True Vine, which is Jesus Christ. As we bear fruit, as our lives are a living testimony of the goodness of God, He is glorified. As He is glorified, many are drawn to Him.

CULTIVATING THE SOIL

So, just how are we to cultivate the soil? How are we to make it just right for the hundred-fold harvest? We begin with spending more time with God. He is more than interested in all that we do. If it were not so, He would never have sent Jesus as the Atonement for our sins. Taking the time to find out more of what God has to say, as opposed to some reality show on television, exercises wisdom and stewardship. By being good stewards of our time, spending it on things *eternal*, rather than on things *infernal*, we cultivate the soil. As we begin to "ingest" the Word, meditate on it, act on it, we lay the ground work for an excellent harvest. Are you ready for the hundred-fold harvest? Have you laid the groundwork for a bumper crop? Don't get caught short with a field of bad soil. Cultivate the soil so the Word of God can do what He has sent it to do.

CHAPTER NINE

CHAOS AND THE POWER OF THE TONGUE

"But the tongue can no man tame; it is an unruly evil, full of deadly poison." (James 3:8)

Just as the Word of God is the seed that is to be sown, the tongue can be described as one of the tools for sowing. Although the tongue is one of the smallest members of the body, it carries the most impact. With the tongue we have the power to both bless and to curse, all with the same member. James 3:10 states, "Out of the same mouth proceedeth blessing and cursing. My brethren, these things ought not so to be." When we use the tongue for any reason outside of God's will, we open the door to chaos because it cannot be controlled. The Scripture says that no man can *tame* it.

Improper use of the tongue can wreak havoc on a person's life, whether intended or not. There is an old saying that goes something like this: "Loose lips sink ships." A catchy phrase, but it manages to capture the veracity of the consequences of an unbridled tongue. When we examine the scope of lives affected by what has been loosed from our tongues over the centuries, the results are nothing short of phenomenal. Wars have been waged and fought from words that are spoken with the tongue. Countless lives have been lost, families disintegrated, and destinies disrupted, all because of an uncontrollable tongue.

THE POWER OF WORDS

When exercising our speech, it is always better to "measure" our words before speaking. Because death and life are in the power of the tongue (Proverbs 18:21) the words that we speak have the power to influence others. This particularly holds true in the case of parents in the process of raising their children. Most children respond to what they are told, either positively or negatively, depending on the circumstance. For example, if a child is constantly told, "You know, you really get on my nerves," "You bother me," or "You're no good, and you'll never amount to anything!" Guess what? Eventually that child begins to behave in the fashion in which he or she has been prone to hearing. The same applies to adults. If a person hears something long enough, eventually they begin to respond in the manner by which they receive it. They begin to believe what is either being said *to* them or what someone is saying *about* them. When this occurs, if what is being said is of a derogatory nature, it can cause feelings of guilt, anxiety, and in some cases, even depression. The recipient often feels inadequate and reflects these feelings of inadequacy in despondent behavior – all based on the power of words.

James put it this way: "And the tongue is a fire, a world of iniquity: so is the tongue among our members, that it defileth the whole body, and setteth on fire the course of nature; and it is set on fire of hell" (James 3:6). What a scathing commentary! So devastating is the power of the tongue, that it can be compared to the fires of hell. The words that we speak can have such impact as to shape the destiny of others.

So often, in anger we tend to "lash out" at others, mainly out of emotion. Unfortunately, the tongue is most often linked to that emotion, which sometimes causes it to "run" out of control. Because it is driven by emotion, in such instances, it can be linked to *carnality*. Carnality is operating from the flesh as opposed to the spirit. The emotion of anger compels a person to speak without the benefit of forethought. How often have we said something in anger only to regret saying it minutes later? That comes from fleshly impulses without the benefit of forethought. The words that we speak are not carefully measured before speaking them.

Many relationships suffer because of the "malicious" wounding of the spirit based on unmeasured speech. Sometimes words are spoken in anger that often leads to regret, and we find ourselves having thoughts like: "Gee, I wish I hadn't said that," or "I'd give anything to take back what I said." But usually by this time it's too late. The damage has already been done, and more than likely the one for whom the anger is directed is hurt by the words that are spoken. This invites chaos into the relationship. This is all the more reason why we should measure our words before speaking, especially during those angry moments when those fleshly impulses rise up to loosen our tongues.

ANGER WITHOUT SIN

Is it possible to be angry and yet not sin? It is entirely possible to do so, and Jesus is our example in Matthew 21 as He confronts the moneychangers in the temple. "And Jesus went into the temple of God, and cast out all them that sold and bought in the temple, and overthrew the tables of the moneychangers and the seats of them that sold doves" (Matthew 21:12). Jesus exhibited a righteous anger in response to the degradation of the temple. He replies in v. 13, "It is written, My house shall be called the house of prayer;

but ye have made it a den of thieves." He was completely justified in His speech. He said nothing that wasn't true, and His anger was evident by the action taken in the overturning of the tables.

Paul tells us in Ephesians 4:26, "Be ye angry and sin not: let not the sun go down upon your wrath." If you should ever find yourself giving in to such a temptation, be warned that by doing so, you allow the Devil to get a foothold. Paul goes on in v. 29 to say, "Let no corrupt communication proceed out of your mouth, but that which is good to the use of edifying, that it may minister grace unto the hearers." When we speak, it should be for the purpose of exhorting one another, not for the purpose of tearing someone down. It was never God's intention for us to live under the bondage of guilt and condemnation. These are the feelings that are brought to bear when we allow corrupt communication to proceed from our lips. We speak words of death and destruction in the lives of many who are unaware of the impact of ill-spoken words. We sometimes have no idea how harmful our negative speech can be to a person.

A LYING TONGUE

A lying tongue is one of the worst things that a person could possess. Why? Because Solomon tells of seven abominations that the Lord hates, and one of them is a lying tongue (Proverbs 6:16-17). A person that lies is constantly sowing confusion and discord. In the process, a chaotic atmosphere is created, which invites the likes of the Evil One to perform works of deceit and destruction. The Bible clearly tells us that Satan is the father of all lies (John 8:44), and when we tell lies, it is a reflection of him. It's no wonder that lying is an abomination to God: it reminds him of Satan.

A lying tongue is corrupt. It has but one purpose, and that purpose is to deceive. It is born out of the wickedness of the heart because out of the abundance of the heart the mouth speaks. Luke 6 v. 45 reads, "A good man out of the good treasure of his heart bringeth forth that which is good; and an evil man out of the evil treasure of his heart bringeth forth that which is evil: for of the abundance of the heart his mouth speaketh."

So just what is it that compels a person to lie? What is it that drives them to the conclusion that lying can somehow improve a particular situation? In some cases, *fear* causes one to lie. It could be the fear of having a particular sin exposed that perhaps threatens to damage one's career or reputation. Sometimes, it's the fear of losing one's life compels a person to tell a lie. This was the case with Abram upon entering Egypt. His wife, Sarai, being a woman of such beauty, he feared would result in his being killed, if Pharaoh knew that Sarai was his wife. He feared for his life so, that he instructed Sarai to tell the Egyptians that she was his sister. Fear prompted Abram to lie in order to save his own life. It became the common denominator of "choice." He could have chosen to tell the truth, but instead allowed fear to influence his decision. As a result, the Scripture says that Pharaoh was plagued because of Sarai (Genesis 12:17). Pharaoh, being led by the lie that had come from Abram's lips, suffered because of the *deception.*

Think of the times that you have been deceived, all because of a lie. Sometimes, the deceit that is born out of a lie can have a crippling effect on our trust. It's not easy to trust a person that has lied to you, simply because the belief is, if it's done once – it can be done again! Most often, this is the case. It's like the story of "The boy who cried wolf." After so many lies, immunity is built up against them. Even if a person is sincere in what they are trying to convey, if that person has a reputation for lying, the words are likely to fall upon deaf ears.

A lying tongue diminishes a person's character. Because he cannot be trusted, he cannot be respected. The deception of a lying tongue, and those who practice it, create chaos at every turn, bringing confusion and dismay to the hearer. Lives take tumultuous turns based on the foundations of lies. In fact, to entertain a person that habitually lies is like being in the presence of a serpent. Just like a serpent, the person that lies is unpredictable. He could strike at any time, spewing out his deadly venom of deceit and trickery. As people suffer, and lives are disrupted, a lying tongue is partially to blame. Many afflictions are brought on because of lies. Proverbs 19 v. 5 says, "A false witness shall not be unpunished, and he that speaketh lies shall not escape."

SPEAKING WORDS OF LIFE

Because both cursing and blessing comes out of the tongue, we have the power to bless someone with the words that we speak. The most common way to bless someone is by greeting him in a cheerful manner. Phrases like, "Have a blessed day," or "God bless you," are familiar and yet simple ways in which we can speak words of life into others. Sometimes a person could be going through a particularly rough time and just the simple utterance of a phrase like: "God bless you" could have a profound effect on them at that moment. Maybe that person is struggling with an issue at home and may feel that God is distant. Just the hearing of those words could be enough to ignite a "spark" within them as a reminder that God hasn't forgotten them.

Speaking words of life into someone is as simple as telling them what the Word of God says about their particular situation. Many people are searching for answers, but unfortunately are seeking in the wrong places. Since the Word of God has transforming power within itself, as we learn it, and begin to *speak it*, not only will we be blessed, but those who hear it will be blessed in return. Remember, the tongue is a sowing instrument. The seed that is sown is the Word of God.

The harvest that comes from this seed has the potential to produce much fruit. So, as we engage with others in our daily activities, it is good to study the Scriptures regularly, so whenever a situation arises, we will be able to respond according to the will of God. That's exactly what Jesus did. For every situation He faced, He always gave an answer based on the Word. Why? Because it is truth and it has transforming power. There will be times when we come across someone who is hurting inside, but may not show an outward appearance of such. As the Spirit of God indwells the believer, he or she may be given a "Word" to speak into the life of that person. Remember, the Spirit searches the heart, even the deep things of God. I Corinthians 2 v. 10 states, "But God hath revealed them unto us by his Spirit: for the Spirit searcheth all things, yea, the deep things of God." When you are in tune with God, the Holy Spirit will guide you in what to say, and when to say it.

In the Old Testament, it was a common practice for the elders of a family, notably the father, to bless the other members of his family. This usually began with the eldest son and carried down to the youngest member. We should bless our children in that same respect today because of what they are up against in the world. There is power in blessing, and the story of Esau and Jacob is a good example. Many families today are missing out on the blessings of God because there is no one present to "pronounce" blessings over their families as the patriarchs did in the Old Testament.

There's something about speaking the Word of God that exudes confidence and reassures the speaker that God can in fact be trusted to be faithful to His Word. By His Word the world came to be, and by His Word, all things are upheld. It is no wonder we get such self-assurance in knowing that God will do what He says. It is no wonder that we are encouraged by the words of the preacher on a Sunday morning. It's not the preacher that excites, nor encourages, or invigorates the soul. But it truly is – the Word of God.

CHAPTER TEN

THE SPECTER OF SPIRITUAL WARFARE

"For we wrestle not against flesh and blood, but against principalities, against powers, against the rulers of the darkness of this world, against spiritual wickedness in high places." (Ephesians 6:12)

Long before the annals of human history were recorded, a war was taking place in the heavens. It was a war that would some day manifest itself within the earth realm, and inflict massive casualties on a scale of immeasurable proportions. It was a war that began in open rebellion against the rule and authority of the One Supreme Being of the universe, who is God. The scope of the rebellion would have such far reaching implications as to not only alter the world as it had been created, but to transcend time and eternity in a conflict so devastating as to stagger the imagination. That war is real, and it exists today.

There are countless numbers of casualties that have been attributed to this war, and man is caught between the crossfire of this conflict; this insurrection to authority that began with an angelic being who wanted to be like God.

His desire and will, so intense, that he persuaded over one-third of the angels in heaven to follow him in his quest. His name? Lucifer. Having once been adorned in heavenly places, constantly in the presence of God, in one fatal decision, had now become an enemy of the Most High God. Lucifer's intentions were clear from the beginning. Isaiah 14:13-14 records the will of this angelic being, in a series of statements that clearly defined his objectives. Verse 13 reads, "For thou hast said in thine heart, I will ascend into heaven, I will exalt my throne above the stars of God: I will sit also upon the mount of the congregation, in the sides of the north:." There were three "I will" statements in that verse alone. Verse 14 reads, "I will ascend above the heights of the clouds; I will be like the Most High." Because of his rebellion, Lucifer, along with one-third of the angelic hosts, were judged by God, and as a result, were cast down from heaven into the earth realm. This is the place where God decided that He would create man. But God didn't just create man for the sake of creating something. When He created man, He created him in His image (Genesis 1:27). Not only did God create man in His own image, but He also gave him dominion over the earth (Genesis 1:28), and crowned him with glory and honor (Hebrews 2:7).

The creation of man was God's *masterpiece*. Although man was created a little lower than the angels (Psalms 7:5), God's favor was apparently with him. This angered Lucifer to no end, whom by this time had come to be known as Satan, the prince of demons, ruler of darkness, Accuser of the brethren, and the chief adversary of God. The stage has now been set for the most consequential battle of all time. Man, crowned with glory and honor by God, becomes the object of Satan's retribution toward God. In all of his fury, the supernatural being called Satan would now unleash the multitudes of demonic forces upon all of earth, and God's unsuspecting creation – man.

So divisive and so destructive are the battle plans for this war that they are unmatched by any army that has ever existed. The strategies are supernaturally conceived and are designed for maximum effect. With targets identified, the enemy of God seeks to destroy His creation by using unconventional tactics, the likes of which the world has never seen. Unlike conventional warfare, the weapons of this war are not carnal. They are of a supernatural nature. Both deadly and effective, these weapons have been known to lay entire continents to waste in the wake of their use.

Wherever unleashed, the result is always devastating. Homes are infiltrated, relationships severed, and families often destroyed. In the wake of the devastation, as with most wars, there is always the "stench" of death; the ever present reminder of this cosmic chaos. The death that takes place in this war is of a spiritual nature. The death of hopes, dreams, possibilities, and futures litter the battlefield in this all out struggle for the souls of humanity. The repercussions of the battle echo from eternity past to times present, sounding the clarion call to arms! Locked into this intense struggle against supernatural opposition, man, left to himself, is utterly defenseless – lying in wait to be consumed by the Adversary.

But who will answer the call to arms? Who will champion the position of authority that God bestowed upon His masterpiece? There is only One who is qualified, One who is capable of mounting an offensive designed to dispel and disrupt the evil intent of the enemy. In fact, yes – even to destroy the works of the Devil! He is the God-Man, the Lord, Jesus Christ. He is the great equalizer, the Firstborn among many brethren (Romans 8:29), and He is all powerful (Matthew 28:18).

A CHAMPION ARISES

He is the one that was prophesied in Genesis 3:15 that would bruise the head of the serpent, who is Satan, also known as the Serpent of old. Being the Firstborn of every creature, this meaning having *preeminence*, or *highest ranking* over creation, Colossians 3:16 tells us that "For by him were all things created, that are in heaven and that are in earth, visible and invisible, whether they be thrones, or dominions, or principalities or powers: all things were created by him and for him."

Having stated earlier that His coming was prophesied, Isaiah 7 v. 14 had this to say: "Therefore the Lord himself shall give you a sign; behold, a virgin shall conceive, and bear a son, and shall call his name Immanuel." The name Immanuel translated means, "God with us." Yes, God Himself would enter this conflict on behalf of His creation in the guise of human flesh (John 1:14) to bring order out of chaos, to restore the authority that He had given to man, and to provide him with sufficient means to repel the onslaught of a most lethal and formidable foe.

While on the earth, He was persecuted, mocked and scorned for His claims of Deity. Having been crucified on a cross, pronounced dead, then buried, Jesus arose on the third day. Having all power in heaven and earth (Matthew 28:18), He made an open show of the principalities and powers which had come to plague mankind. *"And having spoiled principalities and powers, he made a show of them openly, triumphing over them in it"* (Colossians 2:15). Having done this very thing, He effectively "neutralized" the enemy. He had beaten him at his own game. Satan never saw what was coming! He never imagined that God Himself, wrapped up in the Person of His Son, the Lord Jesus Christ, would be so mindful of man that He would in essence "step down" from heaven to come to his rescue.

The plan was brilliant; conceived even before the foundations of the world were established: authored by God Himself. It called for the expulsion of Lucifer from heaven, and a means of redemption for mankind. But why would God need a plan of redemption so soon after Lucifer's expulsion? Because Lucifer had become corrupt, and anywhere he goes he corrupts. This is the reason why man needed a champion, a Savior who not only understood the enemy's strategy, but could relate to man's weaknesses by way of his humanity.

KNOW YOUR ADVERSARY

As a soldier in a war, any good field commander would know that the key to being victorious in battle is first to learn your opponent. It always helps to know who you are facing, in terms of enemy strength, weaponry, and tactics. Our adversary is Satan. He is cunning and ruthless, and will stop at nothing in his quest for destruction. He is illusive; having been engaged in this war for some time now, his expertise and prowess is formidable. There are no rules governing his sense of "fair play" because there is no "fairness" in him. He is wicked and the epitome of evil. He possesses power over the wicked, and they in fact are his children (Acts 3:10). He is referred to as the god of this age (2 Corinthians 4:4), blinding the minds of non-believers and blocking the truth of the Gospel. He is fierce in his determination (Luke 8:29), and capable of possessing human form (Luke 22:3). He is powerful in that he is also known as the "prince of the power of the air" (Ephesians 2:2), and has influence over the children of disobedience. Although Satan is powerful, he is at the same time, cowardly. If there is resistance to him, he will flee (James 4:7). He tempts man to sin (Genesis 3:1-7), and he also attempts to sift him (Luke 22:31). He ensnares (I Timothy 3:7) or sets traps for the purpose of destruction because he is a murderer (John 8:44). He is deceitful (2

Corinthians 11:14), and can transform himself into an angel of light. He is a master of disguise, and can be undetectable until it's too late. One of the biggest deceptions of Satan is to get others to believe that he doesn't exist. This belief creates chaos because it dismisses the consequences of hell, and it allows the devil to run rampant.

DEMONS ARE REAL

Demons are evil spirits who have given their allegiance to Satan. They, like Satan, are powerful and have been known to possess human beings (Matthew 8:28-29). They are unclean (Matthew 10:1), and instigate deceit. They have been known to receive sacrifice (I Corinthians 10:20), and have the ability to overcome men (Acts 19:13-16). Apparently, they recognize Christ, as recorded in Mark 1:23-24. The text reads, "And there was in the synagogue a man with an unclean spirit; and he cried out, Saying, Let us alone; what have we to do with thee, thou Jesus of Nazareth? Art thou come to destroy us? I know thee who thou art, the Holy One of God."

Yes, demons are real, and they most certainly recognize Jesus as the Holy One of God. The question is do we recognize them for who they are? Just like their father, the Devil, part of their power lies in deception. As long as they are believed to be non-existent, they are free to torment man at his own peril. Much of what we see today in the form of sickness and disease can be attributed to demonic activity. Mark 1 v. 34 reads, "And he healed many that were sick of divers diseases, and cast out many devils; and suffered not the devils to speak, because they knew him." And in Matthew 4:24 it states, "And his fame went throughout all Syria: and they brought unto him all sick people that were taken with divers diseases and torments, and those which were possessed with devils, and those which were lunatic, and those that had the palsy; and he healed them." Then there was the case of the man dwelling among the tombs, in Mark chapter 5. According to Scripture, no man could bind him, even with chains (Mark 5:3). The Bible says that night and day he was in the mountains and in the tombs crying and cutting himself with stones (v. 5).

This was clearly a case of demon possession, and Scripture tells us that Jesus called the demons out of him. The man happened to be possessed by many, and they even identified themselves as legion. Most importantly, in this case also, the demons recognized Jesus and submitted to His authority over them.

AVOIDING DEMONIC OPPRESSION

The best way to avoid demonic oppression is to stay in the presence of God. How do you do that? Stay in the Word. Meditating on the Word of God, combined with prayer, will cause the devil to flee. You see, the Word of God is diametrically opposed to Satan's agenda. The Word, when properly administered, erects a wall of resistance that the devil cannot penetrate. Other tangible means of resistance come in ways such as avoiding activities that support *witchcraft*. These activities may include such things as palm readings, séances (meetings with spirits, talking to the dead), and experimentation with Ouija boards, tarot card readings, and astrology. These are all forms of divination, and the Bible is clear on the meaning of such things. These are considered to be forms of "occult" practices that attract evil spirits. If you are a Christian and are dabbling in these practices, stop immediately! You are being deceived by the Evil One and his objective is to destroy you!

ANGELS, OUR ALLIES

In this war of the spirit, God has given us allies. Because Christ has been given all power in heaven and earth, the entire sum of heaven's angels have been placed under His command. At any given time, He can summon legions of angels to aid in the defense of God's people. Matthew 26:53 quotes Jesus as saying, "Thinkest thou that I cannot now pray to my Father, and he shall presently give me more than twelve legions of angels?" Angels were created by God to serve Him. As servants of God, they are organized in ranks or orders (Isaiah 6:1-3). They are powerful (Psalms 103:20), holy (Matthew 25:31), wise (2 Samuel 14:17), and can take human form at times (Genesis 18:2-8). Angels serve as ministering spirits to the children of God. They are sent to guide us, provide for, protect and deliver us from harm. They are also comforting spirits that minister to us in times of despair.

DRESS FOR THE BATTLE

An experienced soldier dresses for battle so that he or she won't become a casualty of war. The book of Ephesians describes the armor of God, which is essential equipment for this supernatural warfare. We are told to put on the "whole armor" of God, that we might withstand the "wiles" of the devil (Ephesians 6:11). Verse 12 says, "For we wrestle not against flesh and blood, but against principalities, against powers, against rulers of the darkness of this world, against spiritual wickedness in high places."

The "wiles" of the devil are devices or schemes that Satan uses against us. The "evil day" can be described as a period of trial or adversity; therefore, it cannot be limited to a particular time frame. First of all, we are to be girded with "truth." This comes from the Word of God — His Word is truth. This signifies our "belt." As we wear the belt, the wording of the text suggests that the "breastplate of righteousness" is a piece of the equipment that we already wear. Our righteousness is in Christ. His righteousness covers us by the blood that was shed for us. This is our breastplate. The next items Paul describes are the "shoes." We are to cover our feet with the preparation of the gospel of peace. What does that mean? It means that as Christians we should be prepared to spread the Gospel, and if necessary, to give a defense for it. Next, we have the shield of faith. According to Paul, this shield is used to repel the fiery darts of the enemy. When we encounter trials, some of which put our faith to the test, we are using our shield. The fiery darts of the enemy may come in all forms, but it is our faith that repels his wicked attempts to get to us. Verse 17 of Ephesians describes the "helmet of salvation" and the "sword of the Spirit." The helmet of salvation is to protect our heads in the battle. It is where our thoughts originate, and where we receive information. As long as we know that we have salvation, and keep our thinking in line with the promises of God, we are wearing the helmet of salvation. "Right thinking" keeps the devil out of our minds, and gives him no room to influence us. The final piece of equipment in the armor is the "sword of the Spirit." This is the Word of God. It's probably the single most important piece of equipment. Once you learn how to wield it properly, the devil will be forced to flee in the wake of it! "For the Word of God is quick, and powerful, and sharper than any two-edged sword, piercing even to the dividing asunder of soul and spirit, and of the joints and marrow, and is a discerner of the thoughts and intents of the heart" (Hebrews 4:12).

WARFARE IN THE HOME

Because spiritual warfare essentially revolves around the Word of God, the home is a prime target for warfare.

The family is God's model for relationship. So much of His will is linked to the well-being of the family, primarily because it is the focal point of human existence. The family is where we are taught our first lessons in morality and the existence of God. It is where we derive our first essential lessons of life, and how to function in society. It stands to reason why the enemy's attention would be geared so much toward the family. Because it is the springboard from which God launches His dominion over the earth, it is also a reflection of Him. There is nothing that Satan hates more than a reminder of who God is.

Warfare begins in the home the minute the devil is allowed to put a foot through the door. It may begin with subtleties in the way of disagreements that can lead to arguments. If these conflicts are allowed to linger, without being resolved, then you open the door for Satan to come waltzing into your home to set up partitions. What are these partitions? They are barriers that block the flow of God's Word from working in your life. His Word becomes of no-effect if it is not allowed to penetrate the heart.

When couples argue and can't come to an agreement of some type, one of the first things to happen is they stop communicating. When the flow of communication comes to a halt, the relationship falters. All of a sudden, thoughts and imaginations begin to creep into the mind, suggesting things that are not necessarily so. These *suggestions* often have a satanic origin, as most often they are planted by Satan. How do we know? Because the Bible says he is the father of lies (John 8:44). If you find yourself thinking ill thoughts toward someone, and you know within your heart of hearts that the thoughts are not true, you need to resist those thoughts. Chances are they are coming from the enemy. Ephesians 4:26-27 gives a warning concerning our anger, and what can happen if it is allowed to linger. Paul states in verse 26, "Be ye angry, and sin not: let not the sun go down upon your wrath:" In verse 27 he says, "Neither give place to the devil." When we get angry and hold things in, we become as ticking "time bombs," waiting to explode! Sometimes, the slightest little thing can set it off. That's why we must learn to put on the *helmet* of salvation each day. It is given to us to guard our minds against the attacks of the enemy. We can't afford to "give place to the devil," as Paul said. He only wants to *confuse* our thinking.

A MINDFUL PRESENCE

Since the beginning of human history, Satan has deployed the same strategy of attacking the mind. It's the "command center" of the body. The brain is what sends signals to the rest of the body telling it what to do. If he has control of the mind, then he has control of you. He is very adept in manipulation. Since his ultimate goal is to destroy us or render us non-effective in the Kingdom of God, he attempts to interrupt our thoughts. When Satan is allowed to infiltrate our minds, the end result is always bad. It usually leads to carnality or thoughts in terms of the flesh. These thoughts could lead to things like obsessions or addictions. According to Romans 8 v. 7, the carnal mind is enmity against God, and is not subject to the law of God, neither can it be. The carnal mind simply will not submit to God. When this happens, there is the danger of being turned over to what the Bible describes as a *reprobate* or "worthless" mind. The word worthless comes from the Greek translation which also means "rejected." A worthless or rejected mind is one that is vulnerable to corrupt thoughts. It is born out of a rejection of the truth of God. Romans 1 v. 28 reads, "And even as they did not like to retain God in their knowledge, God gave them over to a reprobate mind, to do those things which are not convenient." When you openly reject God, you fall away from His protective covering. In doing so, you become "fair game" for the enemy. His manipulative prowess is at its peak when he has a reprobate mind to work with. So, whatever you do, remember to keep the truth of God in your hearts and minds, less you be given over to the reprobate mind. It is sure to cause chaos.

CONCLUSION

Spiritual warfare, or *the invisible war*, as it is sometimes referred, is something that affects all of us. It permeates every facet of life and is no respecter of persons. It reaches across ethic boundaries and economic standing. Social status is of no matter for this warfare is about *all* of humanity and has eternal implications.

It is a war that involves angels and demons, supernatural beings that even at present, are warring over the establishment of the Kingdom of God here on the earth. Many casualties have been inflicted, and many prisoners have been taken and placed in bondage. The enemy has ravaged the earth in his quest for dominance.

As this battle royale rages in the unseen, the physical manifestation is made known to us here in the earth realm. We see the effects of "war in the spirit" manifest itself in things such as murder, theft, pornography, child abortion, all forms of sexual perversions, and wickedness of the heart, that is reflective of the devil. The wickedness, coming as a result of the strongholds that have been placed in the minds of those who chose to believe the lie, rather than the truth of God, and therefore find themselves "naked" in battle. They have no covering to repel the fiery darts of Satan. Their minds cannot comprehend "truth" because of its state.

Man's fallen state required atonement before a Holy God. The atonement was made through Jesus Christ, our Lord. The rejection of His sacrifice is to invite chaos to reign in one's life, never to know the absolute joy, and experience the blessings of being in the presence of Jehovah God.

Yes, many have suffered during this war, but we know that the battle is not ours, but God's (2 Chronicles 20:15). He has given us weapons to accomplish His will for the outcome of this battle. The forces of heaven are at our disposal, and He promises never to leave nor forsake us. It's a winning combination that gives us hope, while we are in the midst of *coping with chaos.*

REFERENCES

Demarest, Bruce. *The Cross and Salvation.* Crossway Books, 1997.
Evans, Dr. Tony. *Identifying With Christ.* The Urban Alternative Radio Broadcast, WAVA-FM.
Geisler, Dr. Norman, and Ron Brooks. *When Skeptics Ask: A Handbook on Christian Evidences.* Baker Books, 1996.
Graham, Dr. Billy. *Angels: Ringing Assurance that We Are Not Alone.* Thomas Nelson Publishers, W Publishing Group, Division of Thomas Nelson, 1995.
Holy Bible, King James Version, Thomas Nelson Publishers, 1976.
Holy Bible, New Living Translation, 2004.
Nelson's Compact Bible Commentary. Thomas Nelson Inc., 2004.
New Webster's Dictionary, Expanded Edition. Paradise Press Inc., 2004.
Shelley, Bruce L. *Church History in Plain Language.* Word Publishing, 1995.
Stone, Nathan. *Names of God.* The Moody Bible Institute of Chicago, 1944.
Sumrall, Lester. *Gifts and Ministries of the Holy Spirit.* Whitaker House, 1982.
The Merriam Webster Dictionary. Merriam-Webster Inc., 1997.

The New Strong's Exhaustive Concordance of the Bible.
Thomas Nelson Publishers, 1990.

10/21/08
Honesty Curie
↳ my good friend
~~571~~ 71986-0741
Hme

Thank you Jesus for bringing this soul to me on 10/21/08 at about 7:30 she came to my Hse at a very down & emotional time she help me a great deal, I was able to get up, cunt Jay, we came over & God work threw her & Amen!